The Samaritan Solution

*Loving Our Neighbor
In A Culture Of Addiction*

Shelly Baron

with Steve Buelow

Dedicated to the love of my life:
My partner, my wife, Maureen.

I love you always.

Table Of Contents

*"... and when he saw the man,
he felt compassion for him."*
– Luke 10:33 (NLT)

Introduction

* * *

A Few Good Samaritans

Addiction.

"Aww, *c'mon,* Shelly!" The elder was incredulous. "We don't have those problems in *this* church! Maybe in others that you've attended, but certainly *not here–* and *not now*!"

"And besides, even if we did," he continued, "there's *nothing* we could do about it, anyway."

I wasn't so sure.

He then went on to detail the myriad problems that he believed the congregation *did* have: dwindling resources, lack of volunteerism, health challenges with young and old alike.

Rebellious youth, disinterest in evangelism, arguments and tension between committee and board members. Crumbling marriages, overstressed and underpaid staff, plateaued membership. And lopsided ratios not only of funerals to baptisms, but also of transfers-out to confirmations, and separations to weddings.

More outgo... than income.

My friend went on to cite the dire forecast from the last budget meeting, the ongoing search for passionate Sunday School teachers, Mildred's diabetes and little Jimmy's leukemia.

He spoke of teen pregnancy, the vacancies in critical leadership roles, and the long standoff between the Board of Education and the greater church council.

His voice cracked as he lamented the Robinson's divorce, the increasing demands on the pastor's schedule, and the passing of several prominent and faithful– not to mention generous– members.

And he expressed sincere pain and hopelessness over postponing critical missions and goals of the congregation, based on current financial considerations. "I guess when it rains, it pours," he said softly. "We just have to weather the storm."

Let me say it again: *Addiction.*

That's right. What if all the circumstances this church leader just described weren't the real problems at all? What if they were just mere symptoms, masking a deeper issue within the hearts and lives of those who make up this small and loving component of the Body of Christ?

Is it possible that the financial and relational challenges, the physical and emotional health issues, the depression and rebellion and division could all be rooted in its members' hidden addictions to alcohol, drugs, prescription medications, or food? Or maybe to uncontrollable activities and behaviors such as gambling, shopping, or pornography?

What if under all the laughter, beneath the smiles and the status, below the houses and the cars and the clothes, were really broken hearts and broken homes?

In that case, the "weather-the-storm" strategy is not only a losing proposition, but may become an absolute death knell for the organization and for the families involved.

Closer to home, what if it's more personal than that? Yes, what if addiction is no longer just an issue that's affecting *those* families and *those* people and *those* relationships over there? What if at this very minute, it's taking its toll on *yours*?

What then? Was my elder friend right?

Is there truly *nothing* that we can do?

Specifically, is Scripture really powerless to provide

answers? Must we fight this battle on our own? How do we know what to do next?

The questions are excruciating.

Do we rationalize and look the other way? Do we keep our nose to the grindstone, literally minding our own business? Or do we seek to please and appease God through our own efforts, while we wait for our friend or loved one to hit bottom?

The pain can seem unbearable, and the uncertainty overwhelming. How can we be sure we're in the right? How can we know? Is there even an agreed-upon definition of addiction? And, if so, can we recognize the warning signs? More importantly, as believers, what is our responsibility in the Church, and what does helping our neighbor *really* look like?

While we're at it, who *is* our neighbor, anyway? And just what is our model for dealing with addiction's causes and devastating effects?

Good questions.

Well, not surprisingly, our answers were given in a Temple conversation that took place around 30 A.D. It seems a lawyer of the time was trying to parse words with Jesus, and he got a lesson in loving his neighbor.

You know the story.

The one where an unlucky traveler is mugged, beaten, robbed and left for dead on the side of the road that leads from Jerusalem to Jericho.

It's a story about treating our fellow brothers and sisters with kindness and mercy and compassion. In typical Jesus fashion, our Lord took a complex life issue and boiled it down into a narrative that any child can understand.

A narrative that *we* can understand:

One day an expert in religious law stood up to test Jesus by asking him this question: "Teacher, what should I do to inherit eternal life?"

Jesus replied, "What does the law of Moses say? How do you read it?"

The man answered, "'You must love the Lord your God with all your heart, all your soul, all your strength, and all your mind.' And, 'Love your neighbor as yourself.'"

"Right!" Jesus told him. "Do this and you will live!"

The man wanted to justify his actions, so he asked Jesus, "And who is my neighbor?"

Jesus replied with a story: "A Jewish man was traveling on a trip from Jerusalem to Jericho, and he was attacked by bandits. They stripped him of his clothes, beat him up, and left him half dead beside the road.

By chance a priest came along. But when he saw the man lying there, he crossed to the other side of the road and passed him by.

A Temple assistant walked over and looked at him lying there, but he also passed by on the other side.

Then a despised Samaritan came along, and when he saw the man, he felt compassion for him. Going over to him, the Samaritan soothed his wounds with olive oil and wine and bandaged them.

Then he put the man on his own donkey and took him to an inn, where he took care of him. The next day he handed the innkeeper two silver coins, telling him, 'Take care of this man. If his bill runs higher than this, I'll pay you the next time I'm here.'

Now which of these three would you say was a neighbor to the man who was attacked by bandits?" Jesus asked.

The man replied, "The one who showed him mercy."

Then Jesus said, "Yes, now go and do the same."

Known as the *Parable of the Good Samaritan,* this story has stood the test of time. Everyone gets it; everyone's familiar with it. In fact, we all learned this precious story as little children... right?

Wrong.

You see, until a year or so ago, my copy of the Scriptures didn't have a "new" testament. You could search all day and not find a Matthew, Mark, Luke, or John– or, for that matter, a Peter, Paul, or Mary!

We had no Jesus.

My "church fathers" didn't have names like Augustine of Hippo, Jerome, Tertullian, or Clement of Rome. No, I never heard of Athanasius, Ignatius, or the council that produced the Nicene Creed.

Instead, we had simple men who became great Patriarchs: men with names like Abraham, Isaac, and Jacob, and a Samuel and David thrown in for good measure.

Growing up in the place known as "Borough Park" to outsiders, Brooklyn's Boro Park District is home to over 300 Synagogues, and is one of the largest Jewish communities outside of Israel.

Although raised there by loving parents and passionately Orthodox grandparents, I literally fought my way to Hebrew School five days a week. One thing was for sure– I had never heard of this *good* Samaritan.

Samaritans, maybe... but not good ones.

Although here's the interesting thing: having never read the New Testament, having never heard the parable, somehow I lived it anyway.

And the immortal words of Jesus Christ, *"...now go and do the same,"* echoed through the centuries, rocking *my* world almost two thousand years later.

New York City– 1971. September 10th, to be exact. And I must tell you, it was a *gorgeous* Friday afternoon. As I headed out to catch the train, the sun was overhead, and I knew this was going to be a day to be remembered.

And then life changed.

A young man, unable to walk, is lying in a doorway. My doorway.

No– more accurately, he is *dying* in that doorway. Yes, dying, amongst the hustle and bustle of the Big Apple.

Dying within sight and step of a thousand passers-by. Dying of the choices he felt he had been forced to make, and the company he'd kept.

But mostly, on this day, he's dying of neglect.

And just like everyone else, I wanted to step over him. I could rationalize that I was on my way to an important meeting– that I was all dressed up, with someplace to go.

And he was so dirty... so vulgar... so violent.

Between his groans and his drunkenness and his drug addiction, I told myself there was no use. He was just too far gone.

Besides, I thought, surely someone else would come along and help him. A doctor or nurse, a policeman or fireman. A pastor or priest or rabbi.

Or then again, maybe this was *my* call. Maybe there wasn't anyone else coming. Maybe that afternoon it was just he and I– and if I didn't get involved, no one would.

Just maybe.

Could it be that that's where you are today? Is it possible that it's just you and your loved one– your friend, coworker, or fellow believer? Yes, just you and your "neighbor," alone on your very own road to Jericho?

And if you don't get involved, no one will.

In *The Samaritan Solution,* we'll address these concerns and more from a Biblical perspective.

We'll define addiction from prevailing Scriptural, secular, and clinical views and provide an understanding of what's really going on with your loved one– and, more importantly, what you can do about it.

We'll identify the danger signs that you can use to spot addiction in general, and the common addictions to alcohol, drugs, food, sex, gambling and pornography in particular.

We'll give you confidence that you can act with love and compassion to begin healing the brokenness of spiritual, physical and emotional relationships, and we'll provide a map to avoid the pitfalls, those devastating mistakes that many families make when confronted with the extreme passions that seem to be ever-present in addiction recovery.

And, most importantly, we will leave you with one powerful message: no matter how much pain, no matter how much you've suffered, no matter how *impossible* it seems, you can have your loved one back again.

The way it was before David's drug use destroyed the trust and his reputation. Before the alcohol made Dad violent again. Yes, before Mom's shopping or gambling decimated the budget, and before Mary's food addiction and smoking stole her health. Before the painkillers and pornography.

Before things fell apart.

If these are concerns that you have today, for yourself or a loved one, in your home or workplace or house of worship, then I believe that it is no coincidence that you're holding this book in your hands today.

It is our sincere belief that *The Samaritan Solution* can also be the answer– the solution– to the struggle that's consuming you.

Part I:
The Jericho Road

"They stripped him of his clothes, beat him up, and left him half dead beside the road."

Chapter 1

*   *   *

Scenes On The Path To Prosperity

Packed like sardines...

The atmosphere in the terminal was electric. The energy so thick, you could cut it with a knife. One of the biggest travel days of the year.

If nothing else, for someone like me who has spent an entire lifetime observing, mentoring, and guiding others, Chicago's O'Hare International Airport usually offers the potential for some unique and interesting conversation.

But on this particular afternoon, something seemed amiss.

A thread of tension, of apprehension... a quiet uneasiness that seemed to wind throughout the waiting area.

People were on edge.

I checked my boarding pass one more time as I struggled to hear the announcement that was broadcast over the public address system.

To no avail. Not this day.

This was the advent of the Spring Break period, and the auditory volume that accompanied the ebb and flow of tens of thousands of harried travelers drowned out any chance of hearing the gate attendant's latest statement.

It didn't matter; I soon got the message.

Literally seconds later, as the moans and groans spread through the crowd that was assembled for departure, it became apparent that our flight was being delayed– again.

Spending an hour on the sidelines in a major U.S. airport is like possessing a looking glass into the country's soul– a microcosm of everything that is good, or bad, about America.

Further, life governed by the Transportation Safety Administration typically operates at two speeds:

There's the TSA speed, and then there's yours.

And, not surprisingly, whether traveling for business or pleasure, few of us are looking for ways to add to the time it takes to get from Point A to Points B, C, and D.

Need proof?

Just ask yourself how often you've accepted the airlines' offer to swap your current tickets in favor of switching to a later flight. For most of us, not even bribery will do the trick.

And this flight was no different.

Business travelers everywhere, trying to get in one more call, one more proposal, one more deal before the long weekend.

And stress, by the planeload.

The first casualty of this self-induced anxiety is often patience. Kindness tends to be a close second, with compassion right on its heels.

And this becomes a real problem– especially if addiction is involved.

You see, many who live life in the fast lane tend to develop an unbalanced interest in self. They are simply too busy to notice that their friend or neighbor or loved one is in serious trouble.

Then there are others who may notice, but who are too self-absorbed to care, especially regarding a mere acquaintance, the friend of a friend, a coworker, or the stranger in the next seat over– yes, even the one on the plane whose very elbow will soon meet their own.

Other times, it's even more personal.

The true movers and shakers may be too consumed to notice the subtle changes in *their own* health and habits, and their increasing dependency on substances and activities that, more and more, are controlling both their public and private behavior.

Yes, they are on the path to prosperity, their own personal Jericho road. Cruising 90 miles an hour with the wind at their backs, they are completely unaware of the signs that point to danger ahead in their careers, their health, their relationships, or in the lives of those they love the most.

Gathered away from the business class that afternoon, there were also hundreds of children, with additional hundreds of parents, all seemingly headed to Florida for vacation.

If only you could have seen it: life and vitality poured from those kids!

The memories from decades past washed over my mind. Oh, to be a thousand miles from school! Oh, to have ten days in the sun! Oh, to get away with great friends and loving family– and oh, to have *no teachers!*

Full of excitement and enthusiasm, and engaged in life, they were talking and texting a mile a minute, and making their parents... proud?

Well, actually, no.

It seemed that all this life and all this vitality– the happiness, energy, excitement and enthusiasm– yes, all the laughter, and all the lightheartedness, was making their parents *angry!*

Yes, angry. Imagine that.

Anger for expressing life.

Anger for enjoying relationships.

Anger for being young and free and filled with passion and vision for the future, even if, for the moment, that vision was no deeper than a tentative appointment with a famous mouse named Mickey in Orlando.

And to think that just a few short years ago, these angry adults would have been bursting at the seams with a similar joy, a childlike energy and enthusiasm that marveled at the simplest pleasures.

So what happened?

I looked into the eyes of each of these grownups. They were exhausted. Some looked ill, and many were obviously overweight. All were completely and totally wiped out.

At that moment I was sure that, for many of these families, this would certainly be a vacation not soon to be forgotten– though possibly for all the wrong reasons.

What is it about America, I thought, that has led so many to strive so hard for things that don't really matter? Is it possible, given their anemic condition, that any of these well-meaning people would even be capable of recognizing a deadly addiction in the life of a friend or loved one?

Moreover, could they ever see the signs in themselves?

And, if so, would they possibly have the strength and endurance that is required for recovery?

While I waited, I would turn these questions over in my mind again and again.

I wondered if it were possible that the *path to prosperity* has really led our nation down the *road to addiction*. And, most importantly, I questioned who would carry on the important work of recovery in an age when people are too busy or tired to either notice or care.

Yes, this is a real and significant challenge– because lives are on the line.

Gosh! After all that, now even I felt worn out!

The flight from Logan earlier that morning had been reasonable enough, departing right on schedule at 7:10 A.M. Still, I hadn't slept much the night before and was feeling a strange combination of nervous excitement and *sheer terror* as the truth of this move began to set in.

Here I was, leaving my island sanctuary on Martha's Vineyard. Leaving the small paradise that my wife, Maureen, and I had created together over a period of eighteen years, and leaving behind the incredible practice that we had built together. Yes, here I was, leaving thousands of friends and associates and patients that we loved dearly.

And actually, I think I handled all of that pretty well... if only that had been the extent of it. Yes, if only.

You see, there's something else I need to tell you— one other matter you need to know. For it wasn't just the home or the lifestyle or the culture I would miss, nor my practice or friendships.

No, this trip would change my life far beyond the loss of any material possessions or relationships, and far beyond my professional network. For on this trip, you must understand, I was also leaving behind the one thing that I valued the most:

I was leaving behind Maureen... forever.

Oh my.

All the memories and emotions, the tears and the triumphs, the successes and failures and dreams that we shared. Seventeen years my junior, she had completed me in ways few men will experience this side of heaven.

Indeed, we were the earthly poster children for the Scriptural definition of marriage. God's "joining together" of man and woman, the literal fusion of our lives and beings. In us, two became one— physically, mentally, emotionally, and spiritually.

Now my mind was whirling, the emotions blocking out the

volume of thousands of weary travelers as I pondered the events of the past week. Just three days earlier, I had walked the six acres of our property with Maureen for one final time... as I scattered her ashes in all our favorite places.

The tall grass where the baby peacocks nested with their mothers, the fountains at the wading pool that refreshed our spirits on so many moonlit walks, and the marsh that we had carefully preserved to guarantee each successive generation of ducks, herons, and swans.

Yes, I know the pain of addiction.

My own Jericho road, my own path to prosperity, has been marked throughout by abuses that, at one time or another, cost me almost everything.

Here was a trail strewn with addictions to alcohol, drugs, smoking, and gambling.

And, yes, also to food– the same addiction that killed my wife.

PICK YOUR POISON

Now, if you are reading this, you know this isn't just my story. It is, to a certain extent, your story as well.

It's been said that everyone knows someone who is suffering from the effects of one addiction or another. It may be the obvious physical destruction associated with drugs or alcohol– and in fact, when most people hear the word addiction, this is what they have in mind: drugs and alcohol.

But that's just the tip of the iceberg.

Tens of millions more are living and dying with more subtle and long-term physical consequences, the result of diseases that are associated with food addiction and smoking– illnesses such as heart disease, obesity, anorexia, bulimia, cancer, stroke, and diabetes.

Or maybe it's the mental and emotional devastation caused by activities like gambling or pornography, behaviors that tear families and relationships to shreds.

And now, today, here we come into this arena, into this mass of personal disaster, with the story of *The Good Samaritan.*

Of all the topics we could attach to this little parable of Jesus, I suppose none may be more volatile. In fact, over the entire course of my lifetime, never have I seen any affliction that can cut so close to the bone, and come to dominate and destroy the relationships where it is involved.

In fact, there is often disagreement within families as to what addiction even is, not to mention its causes and solutions. Always explosive, incredibly ugly, it devastates families and finances, and trashes health and careers. And along the way, it alienates its victims, leaving them feeling hopeless to face this alone.

Now, Believer, you must hear this:

In *First Corinthians,* Scripture says, "The temptations in your life are no different from what others experience." In other words, we suffer from things that are common to all humanity.

I hope you got that, because it is a statement that you can and must put in the bank.

Whatever it is you are going through– whatever you have tried in the past, regardless of the pain, the shame, the guilt or embarrassment, no matter how isolated and desperate you feel– you are not alone. Many others are experiencing the very same things.

Addiction in America is common.

More common than you know.

Before you read any further, let me make sure that you understand what this book is about. *The Samaritan Solution* is not a religious work. It is not a doctrinal statement, nor is it a product nor proponent of any denominational system.

This is a book about a devastating illness that will affect four out of five families in your church, your synagogue, your neighborhood, or your workplace.

Very likely, it is already affecting you.

Addiction is rampant in our country, if for no other reason than that there are just so many substances and activities to which one can become addicted. Yes, America offers a feast for the senses. We live in a culture that celebrates its excesses and its out-of-control celebrities.

If I can't get you a drink, maybe I can offer you a smoke.

If not one, then another.

Are you broke? Gambling may be just your ticket to riches.

Lonely? Pornography could help.

Suffering from a lack of self-esteem or self-worth? Some expensive-looking jewelry and a new wardrobe will have you feeling better in no time.

Temptation is everywhere, promoted by marketers who will earn a profit and by governmental agencies that will collect a tax.

Yes, when it comes to addiction, America is absolutely the "Land of Opportunity." There is something for everyone.

At one time or another, most of us have witnessed or experienced the destructive toll that drug or alcohol abuse can wreak on both individuals and families.

We've seen compulsive sexual activity bring down powerful political leaders, or uncontrollable gambling ruin the reputations of popular sports and business figures.

We've visited the hospitals and nursing homes where friends and relatives struggled with complications and diseases associated with the use of prescription drugs, or the long-term abuse of tobacco.

At other times, we watched as Uncle Tony got bigger and bigger, while our fragile coworker, Jill, simultaneously wasted away. Obviously, standing by helplessly was not a solution for either of their food addictions.

We cry out, "Why are our loved ones killing themselves? Why don't they all just stop?"

Answer: because they can't. At least, not alone.

Now, here's the really sad truth:

Years before their issues made headlines, before the marriage ended, before the public embarrassment or the health complications, you or I or someone suspected a problem.

Addiction, in all its forms, brings with it negative behavioral changes that are impossible to miss, especially if you know what to look for.

That said, what's next?

When behavior begins to go wrong, is there help available? And if so, can those in the middle of an emotional meltdown find it before it's too late, before there is serious difficulty, before our loved one breaks the law and is incarcerated, or before they injure themselves or others?

Before you need to bury them?

Yes, addiction kills.

And unfortunately, many who are smack-dab right in the middle of it refuse to call it what it is. You see, there is a very negative stigma associated with the word *addiction.*

In fact, for decades, there has been a great division in our society in the attempt to define the cause of addiction. The arguments have had the effect of separating us into what has essentially become two camps:

The first camp says that addiction is the outcome of bad choices, rebellious and selfish behavior, and poor moral character.

The second camp says that addiction is a medical condition, an illness or disease to which the addict was predisposed and had little choice.

We will cover this extensively throughout the remainder of the book, but suffice it to say here that a family's point of view will typically determine its initial response.

They might likely berate or attempt to punish an individual who is seen as irresponsible or hurtful. But would using anger, shame or guilt be the appropriate response with a family member who has become ill?

You can see the difference.

It's no secret that much of our criminal justice system is set up to operate using the punishment model. Without a doubt, it is the accepted course of action, though it is worth asking from time to time that we apply some metrics to the method.

In other words, how's it working?

Have you noticed a remarkable drop in drug and alcohol use since the "war on drugs" began, or is substance abuse more prevalent today than ever?

Has pornography stayed consistent over the last generation, or has it proliferated into every corner of our society to fill the insatiable demands of sex addiction?

With all our technology, with all the studies, with hundreds of millions of dollars in research grants for health sciences– are more or fewer people suffering from the symptoms of food addiction such as obesity, anorexia, high blood pressure, diabetes, and heart disease?

The answers are certain.

When it comes to addiction, it seems the punishment and ostracization method seldom works. Shame and guilt tend to reverse the intended effect. Alienation and abandonment simply cause heartache and broken relationships.

To understand why, it may be helpful to distance ourselves momentarily from the emotional roller coaster that accompanies addiction in the lives of those we care about.

In other words, let's get clinical.

As difficult as it may be to pull yourself away from the fear, anger, and frustration that you are feeling, it is important that you know that *all* addiction follows a similar pattern.

Also, recent advances in medical science and technology have identified hormonal and chemical changes that affect brain activity in persons suffering from addictions, and– here's a flash– not just when they are using.

Yes, you heard that correctly.

The addict's brain has undergone changes affecting the neurotransmitters serotonin and dopamine that regulate our moods and our ability to sense and experience pleasure.

Now, here is what absolutely floors most family members at the outset:

Interestingly, it appears that these brain changes are common to addicts, *regardless* of the substance, behavior, or activity that is causing the problem. This means that a person struggling with food addiction, gambling, or pornography is just as likely to experience them as an alcohol or drug abuser.

To clarify, when a pathological gambler's fix is not available, when a food or pornography addict cannot consume their substance or activity of choice, and when a compulsive shopper cannot shop, they exhibit physical withdrawal symptoms that are astonishingly similar to those experienced by individuals who are dependent on alcohol and drugs!

The implications of these findings weigh heavily in favor of the argument that addiction is an undesired medical condition, as opposed to the well-deserved outcome of an individual's conscious choices, rebellious spirit, and poor judgment.

Now, please understand, I am not saying that the individual hasn't contributed to the mess that they find themselves in. Nor am I suggesting they not be held accountable in cleaning it up. I am merely pointing out that, more often than not, there were already serious issues there to begin with, issues they were trying desperately to control.

It is important to understand that, in the beginning, the use of any substance or activity in an addict's life is typically an attempt to reduce pain or discomfort of one sort or another.

That's it... pain.

Their addiction may begin as an attempt to self-medicate a hidden condition as serious as depression or schizophrenia, or as simple as a desire to avoid the pressure of their peers.

They weren't out to ruin their life or the lives of their friends and loved ones. They simply felt better or less stressed when they were using.

Period.

Along the way, however, several lines were crossed.

The first, in which they could no longer feel good without the substance or activity, and the second, where they no longer feel good at all.

I suppose there are several reasons that you may have picked up a book entitled *The Samaritan Solution.*

It could be that you have family living in Israel's West Bank and thought this may provide an interesting political answer to the ongoing struggle.

But I doubt it.

Or maybe you're in charge of your house of worship's youth

group, and are always looking for stories that could help instill a spirit of love, helpfulness, and kindness into the children's otherwise 'me'-focused lives.

Though I don't believe that either.

No, more than likely, this book found its way into your possession from a caring friend who knew what you and your family are going through. Or maybe it jumped out at you while you were innocently passing time in your local bookstore, or making use of *your* flight delay by perusing the shelves in the airport gift shop.

I guess it's even possible that you found it at my website, searched it on Amazon, or ran across it while Googling the word *addiction.*

In any event, I believe you are reading this book for one of three reasons:

First, you are concerned about a friend or loved one, and are looking for confirmation of the problem.

Second, you already know that you're dealing with addiction, and want to know what, and what not, to do next.

Third, you are looking for hope and practical advice, written in a down to earth manner that is understandable and immediately actionable.

In any event, you'll find what you're looking for here.

Now, on the other hand, I suppose I could have written a textbook about the divisions that exist in clinical theoretical approaches to the diagnosis and treatment of addiction.

Next, I could have argued the positives and negatives from each point of view, beginning with university professors who have million-dollar research grants and then moving on to general practice family physicians, behavioral scientists, psychiatrists, economists, and criminal justice experts.

Then I could have laid out the countless definitions of

addiction that have been promoted through the years by authors and teachers and social work professionals, and backed that up with data from the National Survey on Drug Use and Health (NSDUH) and the Substance Abuse and Mental Health Services Administration (SAMHSA).

Finally, while I was at it, I suppose I could have driven deep into the BioPsychoSocial model of addiction, and then knocked it home with criteria from the Diagnostic and Statistical Manual of Mental Disorders (DSM-IV).

In fact, just for fun, we could have done it all in Latin.

And, in the end, what would all those words have profited you?

If you said, "Nothing," you understand the pain of being on the inside. You just want to have some strength, some confidence, some shred of belief to cling to. You want to understand what is happening in your family, and why.

Because, deep inside, you know that right now your son or daughter, your husband or wife, your father, your mother, your neighbor or friend is dying.

And it's breaking your heart.

Now, Believer, I am going to give you hope.

In over forty years, having successfully treated more than nine thousand patients and their families, I have *never* met an addict that could not be helped.

Never. Not one.

AN EQUAL OPPORTUNITY DESTROYER

As I travel, and as I teach on this subject, I am often asked about who is most at risk of becoming addicted.

For example, do doctors and attorneys have a higher rate of alcoholism because of the extreme stress in their careers? Are inner city minorities more likely to abuse street drugs than their suburban counterparts? Do single moms struggling to make ends meet have a higher incidence of gambling?

How big a role does education or income play in food addiction and the eating patterns of our population? What about the Internet and our youth?

Well, there's good news and bad news.

The good news is that such thoughtful questions suggest a fresh page is being turned in the search for information and answers about addiction. This new environment of open dialogue and honesty about a topic that was formerly shrouded in secrecy has created a profound level of awareness. And with awareness comes the possibility of recovery.

After all, in the past, addiction was not a subject respectable people spoke much about. And it wasn't all that long ago that the very mention of the word sent those in the church or synagogue running for the hills.

Like the friend I introduced you to earlier, the last place we would look for signs and devastating effects of addictive behavior was within the community of believers, especially our own.

Yes, of course we knew there were problems– but we figured they were limited to the poor, the violent, the rebellious, or the criminal. And they were certainly confined to neighborhoods far from ours.

The bad news, of course, is that everything we thought we knew about addiction turned out to be wrong.

As awareness has been raised, addiction– along with all its behaviors and consequences– has been exposed in our own homes, and in our families.

It has made front page news in our places of work, and our houses of worship. We see it in the conduct of our politicians, and the lifestyles of our rich and famous.

No, addiction does not discriminate. It is an equal opportunity destroyer.

I was born into a fantastic home– and yet I became addicted. I had loving parents, a wonderful childhood, and every advantage growing up. I married into a powerful family, had influential friends and associates, and met fabulous celebrities and sports legends. And we were all addicted.

The fact is that the alcohol, the drugs, the gambling, the food, and the sex aren't impressed with your title. They don't favor one family, one race, or one creed.

Rich, poor, or in-between, you're all welcome. Black, white, red, yellow or green, hop aboard. Christian, Jew, and Atheist, glad you made it– we've been waiting for you. Nor is it restricted to the Western world.

But here is what is important. Willpower alone won't cut it. Our firm resolve will lead to defeat.

Please understand that, left alone, the outcome is always the same: ruined health, lost potential and destroyed relationships.

Broken bones, hearts, and homes.

Addiction comes to rob its victims of their finances and their health, to destroy their hope and their future, and to steal their vision, their potential and their relationships.

Now, you would think that any illness, behavior, or activity that was that destructive would be easy to spot.

But addiction has an insidious way of sneaking up on its victims. In fact, often disguised as a symptom of something else, seldom does anyone notice when it prepares its attack.

Chapter 2

*   *   *

Falling Amongst Thieves

S tories.

The world is full of stories.

They are what bind generation to generation and bring people of diverse cultures together around common themes. Indeed, a simple story from two thousand years ago is what has literally put us on the very same page today.

You see, throughout the centuries, mankind has shared not only its history, but also its experience, strength, and hope in the form of oral and written testimonies and narratives.

In short, they shared their stories.

And the stories that make the greatest impact– the stories that last– are those that resonate with the listener. Indeed, great stories allow us to be transformed, to be transported in time. They allow us to connect and to be intimately involved. Because, after all, the situations described– the joy, the sadness, the drama– all could have happened to us.

In fact, very often it *has* all happened to us. And that was the point of this first-century parable.

As He laid out this story, Jesus made the point that we can place ourselves in any role we choose. We could be one of the good guys, or one of the bad.

Now, a third grader would certainly tell us that we should act the part of the Samaritan, selflessly taking our time and giving of ourselves to help our fellow man who is obviously in need. Even taking away the religious context, most children will still come to the correct conclusion.

But an adult who is giving an honest answer might well have to acknowledge that, more often than they care to admit, they have been one of the overly pious and preoccupied believers. Yes, the ones in the story who passed by on the other side of the road. We are often too focused on our own concerns to even notice, or too busy to grasp the severity of the situation.

However, there is another reason that this timeless story of *The Good Samaritan* still clicks with us today.

Quite simply, there are plenty of people who can identify with the victim. Indeed, this story sounds like the news at the top of any hour, or the talk around the office water cooler.

People just going about their daily business: traveling on the road to personal success, to recognition, prosperity, and wealth. Yes, traveling their own road to Jericho– only to be blindsided, injured, and sidelined along the way.

Let's face it: if you're feeling a bit beat-up these days, you're not alone. And it's not just the concerns over escalating crime rates.

In fact, the truth is that the percentage of Americans who will be affected by violent crime is quite small– miniscule, in fact, when compared to the number that will experience much more common and unexpected turns in life that have the potential to steal their hopes and dreams.

Economic worries, health issues, and bitter partisan politics seem to have the whole nation on edge. Wars and rumors of wars wrench the hearts and emotions of family and friends in a nation whose sons and daughters are headed overseas.

In our cities, towns, and villages, the stress of company closings and mass layoffs amid rising energy and fuel prices create tension in our neighborhoods and communities.

Higher taxes, lower home equities, and plummeting 401k's.

Yes, there's plenty of trouble to go around.

But as believers, should we be surprised? After all, we've been instructed that life is made of seasons, some of which will contain trouble.

Count on it.

And as seasons come and go, therein lies our hope. Like any cycle, we expect that over time, things will get better. We can handle the clouds, because we know that the sun will shine again. It's just a matter of time.

So, as difficult as it seems, we believe the economy will improve. We can get new jobs, and insurance. The stock market will come back; it always does. And one day, maybe someday soon, the war will end.

Relax... everything will be good again!

Not so fast.

What if there's something else brewing here?

What if, at this very moment, the trouble that has settled into your home *isn't* going away? What if this time it is only going to get worse?

What then?

Well, if you have read this far, you already suspect trouble.

Or maybe you know that it's worse than that. Tensions are long past the boiling point, and this particular relationship in your life has gone really, *really* wrong.

So many questions.

So much confusion.

So many unknowns, and seemingly nowhere to go and no one to ask to get help.

Why is your friend or your loved one behaving like this?

Why are they so angry– and, more to the point, why are they so willing to hurt you?

Could it be their job? Is it their finances? Maybe their health? Are they depressed? Or are those just symptoms of a deeper problem, a condition over which they have absolutely *no* control?

Could it be, in fact, that they are unknowingly on the road to addiction?

Oh my...

Addiction.

It's a word that shakes most people to their core, a word that leaves us feeling scared and helpless.

Yes, addiction and its many related behaviors and consequences always hurts other people. And right now, it may be hurting you– affecting your relationships and every plan you had for your future.

Regardless of how you think it started or how deeply you think it's rooted, addiction is a progressive condition that won't stop with just stealing your loved one's health, trashing their finances, obliterating their personality, and shredding the relationship you share.

No– despite your every effort, that is only the beginning.

Addiction has an end game.

Please hear me:

You need to know that regardless of all your love, notwithstanding all your patience and caring, there is a very strong possibility that this time your loved one may not survive this.

And, as we will learn shortly, the choice of outcomes may actually be yours. The question is, are *you* ready for what lies ahead?

ON THE WAY TO RAGS OR RICHES

By all accounts, the road leading out of Jerusalem's Eastern Gate was filled with potential. Potential payoff... or potential peril.

Leaving at dawn, and winding through a mountainous region on a path overlooking the Jordan River, those in pursuit of first-century commerce could expect to travel an entire day by foot, with their life's fame and fortune balanced carefully on the back of a sure and steady beast of burden.

Seventeen miles to the northeast, Jericho was a lush oasis in the wilderness, beckoning weary travelers and merchants alike.

This ancient city, whose impenetrable walls had come tumbling down under the onslaught of Joshua's famed assault fourteen hundred years earlier, now stood as a testimony to the power, resilience, and wealth of its citizens.

Jericho.

The city of palm trees. The city of fragrance.

Yes, fragrance– at a time and place in history where your desire for an ounce of perfume may cause you to part with an entire year's wages. This was a hub of wealth, a magnet for riches and power. And getting there and home in one piece would likely mean the difference between achieving years of financial prosperity, or sending the children to bed hungry again.

But, certainly, it was not without risk.

Flying over that area today, one can still imagine the precariousness of such a trip. A rocky and winding trail, the mountains west of the Jericho Plains provided many a hiding place from which bandits could launch an ambush on an unprotected and solitary individual.

This was terrain in which the advantage clearly went to the

aggressor. The fear that accompanied the traveler would have grown more overwhelming with each step of their journey– with each turn in the road.

From that vantage point, you could see your destination for miles! Just a few more hours, and all would be well...

Or would it?

For that answer, you'd need to fast-forward a few days.

You see, arriving safely in Jericho with all of your wares still intact was only half the battle, just the first leg of your trip. Yes, the marketplaces would be filled with frenzied activity– music and dancing and chaos– as buyers and sellers played out the game in every imaginable product niche.

Commodities such as grain and flour, tools and pottery and bolts of woven cloth, furniture and jewelry and musical instruments, and animals for work or sacrifice.

Just one problem.

After a week of successful wheeling and dealing, there was still the road home. In fact, the real goal was never getting to the market. No, the real goal was safely traveling the return trip, the seventeen miles that separated you from those you cared about most.

That was the reason you went. That was the road that mattered. And the thieves and robbers that made their living on that path– yes, the same thieves and robbers who watched as you passed a few days earlier with all your merchandise– now watched as you returned.

And they knew that the bags your animal now carried were valuable for a different reason, for they were loaded with the proceeds from the sale of all your goods.

Then, as now, falling amongst thieves could cost you everything.

AMBUSHED

No sane person desires to be victimized.

No one wants to be robbed. We all start out with the best intentions and plans.

We are going to be successful.

We've been taught from childhood that the ticket to a prosperous and happy life is that we need to really apply ourselves.

We need to work hard.

Yes, we need to work *really* hard– oh, and don't forget education!

We need to get a good education, which will lead to a good job where we can work even harder and apply ourselves even more, and then we'll...

Get divorced?

Suffer from high blood pressure and heart disease?

File bankruptcy?

Abuse our spouse and children?

Is that what it's really all about?

Or maybe we can just keep all of this quiet.

Yes, maybe if we look good enough and smell good enough and drive the right cars and live in the right neighborhood– maybe if we have the right friends and the right contacts and are seen in the right places– maybe we can learn to put up a really good public front and just find a way to keep all of our family's skeletons tucked safely away in the closet.

"Now, just hold on a second, Shelly," someone is saying. "Where are you going with this? I really *am not* comfortable with the tone of this anymore. This is starting to seem a little personal. And what does all this have to do with addiction anyway?"

Now, there are two things you need to know.

First, there *is* nothing comfortable about dealing with this subject; and second, you do not have to go through this suffering in silence by yourself anymore.

Like an infection that must be opened in order to heal, addiction is a disease that lives under the surface, and can only thrive when ignored. In fact, there is an old saying that says, "We are as sick as our secrets."

Though this phrase cannot be found verbatim in Scripture, I believe it is Scriptural nonetheless. However, I would like to add one word to the statement, and that is the word "only."

"We are *only* as sick as our secrets."

Meaning it doesn't have to be. The day that we open up and start to shine light on the true nature of our problems is the day that healing and restoration can begin.

The truth is that we don't have to hide. We don't need to be ashamed. We don't need to do this alone.

It has often been said that addiction is a lonely place. We want to keep this hidden; we don't want the world to know. Because of this, millions (yes, millions) of our fellow citizens— our friends, neighbors, relatives, and coworkers— are secretly suffering by themselves.

Suffering while they hide.

Suffering with hopelessness and despair and loneliness.

And that is the saddest part of all. Because addiction is a disease which no one wants to speak about, each family suffers from common and treatable circumstances, all the while thinking they're alone.

To be sure, when it comes to addiction, we are most definitely not alone.

More importantly, there are precautions we can take to recognize the dangers, and to protect ourselves from the ravages of addiction and its related symptoms, those thieves who would rob us of our health, our finances, and our relationships.

So, take a deep breath and understand that you are now among friends.

There is no judgment here, no place for finger-pointing, anger, guilt, shame, or embarrassment. Indeed, as we will soon see, those are the actions and emotions that are most damaging to your loved one's recovery.

No, in this chapter, we are simply going to look at the illness, and recognize it for what it is– the most common and costly disease in the country, secretly affecting almost every family you know.

Yes, you heard correctly. Addiction, in one form or another, is currently affecting virtually every family you know.

PROFILE OF A ROBBER

First, let's clear up what addiction is not.

Addiction is not the use of illicit street drugs like crack cocaine, methamphetamine, PCP, marijuana, or heroin. Addiction is not your friend's enjoyment of the casino, your coworker's viewing of certain movies or websites, your brother's smoking and drinking or your mother's fascination with Rocky Road Double Nut Triple Fudge ice cream.

Though, then again... it might be.

Addiction is a physical, psychological, or emotional dependence on *any* behavior, activity or substance that ultimately affects the moods or actions of the individual, especially when the focus of their addiction is withheld– as when an individual tries to quit.

Addiction is characterized by a progressive series of behaviors– including the increased use and abuse of a substance or activity, followed by frequent attempts to control or stop the behavior, the loss of willpower resulting in frequent relapse, significant degradation of physical, social, psychological and emotional health, and finally submission to a disease that, if allowed to run its course, will ultimately claim the addict's life.

And this progression is true regardless of the substance, behavior, or activity to which one is addicted. Indeed, as we will see, those with addictions to gambling, pornography, and shopping frequently die decades early, and from the very same illnesses and circumstances as do those afflicted with addictions to alcohol, drugs, tobacco, and food.

And once submission to the disease occurs, your loved one needs to use like you and I need to breathe. Yes, there are fleeting moments where they still dream of a healthy life; yes, they may even get nostalgic or depressed longing for how things were or how it could have been.

But those days are gone.

Please know that if your family or your relationships are hurting, it is likely that addiction is in there somewhere. If you or a loved one is being treated for common illnesses such as high blood pressure, cancer, heart disease, obesity, anorexia, bulimia or diabetes, addiction is almost certainly present. In fact, I believe that nearly every illness in the country has its roots planted firmly in addiction.

Every one.

And if you're having trouble with that idea, it is likely that you're operating with an invalid and inaccurate definition of addiction, correlating the word with substance abuse only. Yes, I believe you may have missed the characteristics of addiction that we reviewed moments ago.

So go back and read it.

I'll wait.

Possessing a clear understanding of these attributes is critically important to our discussion, for you see, many of us have become so accustomed to linking the words "addiction" and "drugs" that we lose all sensibility about the connection to every other behavior, substance, and illness.

With this new definition in mind, let's look at the prevalence of addiction in our society. Let's look at that thief that has its eye on your family and finances. And while we do, I hope you will come to understand that the volatile nature and circumstances of addiction that you may be struggling with in your family are very commonplace in our country.

Indeed– and this cannot be stated too many times– addiction and all of its related consequences and destruction are widespread behind the closed doors in the homes of those in your circle of friends, neighbors, relatives, and coworkers.

And yes, even in your church, congregation, or synagogue.

But just in case you thought your problems were different, or that your loved one should just shape up, simply quit, and then everything will be good again, consider these facts:

With an estimated direct cost to our health care system of over a quarter of a *trillion* dollars every year, substance abuse now reaches into every corner of our society.

In the twelve to seventeen age range, one out of three children now reports using drugs. It is estimated that the numbers could be significantly higher, but that those surveyed were afraid of being found out.

In the eighteen to twenty-five age range it's even higher, with over 50% reportedly involved in using drugs. That's one out of every two! So let me ask you, do you know twenty kids in that demographic? Do the math. Still think you're all alone?

And what are the effects of these statistics?

Interestingly, over 80% of all crime in the U.S. is related to drug or alcohol addiction. Alcohol abuse in men increases the chance of partner abuse by 800%. And two-thirds of victims of domestic violence report that alcohol was involved in the incident.

Incredibly, 94% of alcoholics die from complications and illnesses related to their drinking, on average 26 years earlier than their normal life expectancy.

Remember, the definition of addiction is the inability to stop, in spite of the negative effects to one's health, physical or otherwise. If they weren't addicted, if they could just quit, they would.

Unfortunately, many who give up drinking suddenly double up on their smoking. Tobacco use kills 440,000 U.S. citizens annually, and burdens our economic system to the tune of 92 *billion* dollars.

Each year, nearly 35 million people attempt to quit smoking. Less than 7% succeed in abstaining for more than a year, and most start smoking again within days.

Death from smoking-related illness drags the entire family through a very ugly, very painful, and very prolonged process.

Everyone *knows* that if they could just quit, they would.

So, you say the problem in your life isn't drugs or alcohol or smoking. No, those you could live with. In fact, substance abuse would almost be respectable compared to what's going on in your family– embarrassing addictions to gambling, shopping, or pornography.

Are you feeling alone?

Well, recent reports indicate that 86% of American adults have gambled during their lives and 60% do so in any given year. Studies show that those with a gambling addiction are much more likely than others to have problems with drinking, drugs, smoking, and depression. There is also a strong link between suicide and gambling addiction.

If they could just quit, they would.

In 1996, a *Promise Keepers* survey at one of their stadium events revealed that over 50% of the men in attendance were involved with pornography within the seven days preceding the event.

Now, that was the mid-90's, *before* high-speed Internet made it available in virtually every home in America, and practically every mainstream hotel in America put their endorsement on it.

Today, according to recent studies, more than 70% of men from 18 to 34 admit to visiting a pornographic site in a typical month, and over half of all evangelical pastors report viewing pornography in the last year.

According to *Focus on the Family*, 47% of respondents said that pornography is a problem in their home, and it is now cited as a significant factor in two out of every three divorces.

Finally, *Today's Christian Woman Newsletter* reports that 34% of their female readers admitted to intentionally accessing Internet porn in a recent poll, and one out of six women said that they struggled with an addiction to pornography.

Certainly, if they could all just quit, they would.

In fact, the individual *struggling* with addiction is doing just that– they are literally struggling and fighting with addiction.

The drug or alcohol abuser, the smoker, knows that their behavior is killing them. Those struggling with gambling, shopping, pornography, or any other addictive behavior know that their health and relationships are in jeopardy.

They've tried to quit, quite possibly a thousand times– and, at some point, it no longer seems possible to live without whatever serves as the fix.

At this point, death would be less painful than quitting... and it is the option that many unfortunately and unnecessarily choose.

Now, I suppose it is possible that you are still feeling alone, that addiction has landed on your shores but you don't see it anywhere else. So let me offer a bit of news on one more addiction, because I believe it affects nearly 70% of our population.

In fact, as volatile as alcohol and drug abuse cases can be, as draining as it can be to watch a smoker slowly commit suicide, as devastating as the lies and hidden behaviors of gamblers and porn addicts can be, they are not necessarily the most difficult addictions to break– nor are they the addictions with the greatest health consequences to our citizens and our nation.

No, that distinction must go to a form of substance abuse that many Americans are just beginning to acknowledge. And that substance is food.

It's no secret that our country is experiencing an epidemic of health complications associated with excess weight and obesity. The Center for Disease Control recently published a report stating that fully two-thirds of the adult population are either overweight or obese, and for the first time ever, the percentage of those suffering from obesity is *greater* than those who are merely overweight.

Much of heart disease, cancer, diabetes, and stroke can be traced to this one statistic alone. Certainly with a million and one diet programs, and a Curves on every corner, we should have obesity and its devastating health effects on the run.

So what's wrong?

The problem with all addiction is that we actually have to admit that we have a serious problem– and most people don't want to look at their own diet and nutrition in those terms. Further, they certainly don't want to identify the "A" word– addiction– as a likely culprit in the health and life of every overweight and obese friend or family member that they have. Because, well, there may be a bunch of them.

And for sure they don't want to consider it in themselves.

So we cover it up, and food addiction is an easy addiction to hide. We tell ourselves that those who are suffering aren't addicts. No, in fact, they're just jolly.

Jolly?

Yes, they just like their food! They enjoy a good meal. They have a great relationship with their food!

Hmm...

If it's such a great relationship, then why is their food killing them?

Contrary to alcohol and drug abuse in which the physical effects can be seen rather quickly, *food* addiction operates with far more stealth. The physical damage can take years to become obvious, though the internal damage is happening almost from the start.

The morning after an alcohol or drug bender, everyone can see the evidence of a problem. On the other hand, when people are eating improperly, the signs are much less obvious.

The individual shows up on time for work. They answer their door, and greet their guests. Things seem normal. But inside, the damage is building.

And with food addiction, we're not talking about someone who is strung out. No, we're talking about your mother, or your brother, or maybe even *you*.

Now, please understand, I'm not pointing fingers. I was there. I *am* there. I am a food addict who picks up my fight against this disease every morning. And it wasn't until I faced this issue head-on that I got the help I needed, lost 183 pounds, and eventually received answers to *all* of my health issues.

Besides, the overweight and obesity statistics aren't mine, they're from the federal government. And let's not forget that on the other extreme, we have anorexics and bulimics– opposite sides of the same food addiction coin.

You see, the question is not *whether* any of us is eating too much or too little. The question is *why* are we overeating or undereating? And why can't we fix this, despite our own efforts, despite the warnings we've read, despite the last test results?

Unfortunately, most of us have never been told that food addiction is nothing more than a correctable, chemical disorder. It attacks our physical and emotional well being, and causes a myriad of health challenges such as heart disease, cancer, high blood pressure, stroke, and diabetes.

Most of us don't know that some people cannot properly break down refined carbohydrates– their pancreas overreacts, and produces too much insulin, causing glucose levels to plummet, thus driving them to eat *more carbohydrates!*

It's as simple as that, but it's a vicious– and ultimately deadly– circle. I know, because it claimed the life of my wife, Maureen, at the age of fifty-four. And this is particularly troubling because this thief, which steals the lives of so many and causes years of needless anguish and illness, is absolutely 100% treatable.

SNEAK ATTACK

We cannot leave this section without calling your attention to the most insidious trait of this disease. To be sure, if you only take one principle from this book, this would be a good one.

Earlier, I stated that nearly 94% of all alcoholics will die from complications that are related to their disease, and they will die, on average, 26 years earlier than their normal life expectancy. Well then, it would seem to be a simple and rational conclusion that if these individuals could just get sober sooner, they would get their life– and all those years– back.

Think again.

Countless families have attended countless funerals of loved ones who beat alcohol, only to die decades early from some other physical malady.

I have been to more of these events than I care to remember, and each time the relatives and friends, the priests, preachers, and rabbis, eulogize old Sam as a good man who worked hard to overcome his illness.

Yes, he died too soon, the story goes. But at least he died sober.

Or did he?

The truth is, this story neglects to answer the question of *why* these people died so much earlier than they should have. After all, they'd beaten alcohol or drugs or the stimulant of their choice, hadn't they?

How unfortunate that they saved their liver, only to die of heart disease or emphysema or diabetes.

Yes, how unfortunate indeed.

But is it possible that the answer to the question really lies in the fact that our friend, Sam, wasn't really sober after all? That he had merely traded one addiction that could have killed him, for another one that did?

Think back to our earlier definition of the classic characteristics of addiction. It is "a *progressive series* of behaviors." Please, you must hear this, for it is the most misunderstood aspect of the entire subject of dependence.

If you are struggling with addiction, it will not go away.

Without proper treatment, stopping one behavior will simply cause the manifestation of another, and the last state will likely be worse than the first– which, by the way, is also Scriptural, so put it in the bank.

After forty-plus years working with addicts and their families, the signals are pretty easy to spot. All addictions have associated behaviors that play out in a similar but very complex fashion.

And it doesn't much matter what type of addiction is involved– from my point of view, there are red flags that go up everywhere.

So, I often wonder, why can't everyone see them? Why didn't Sam's coworkers notice, or his priest or rabbi? And how on earth could his doctor have missed it?

Good grief!

"Now just wait a minute, Shelly!" someone says. "I see where you're headed with this, and we have a very good doctor! And furthermore, Uncle Bob *did not* die from addiction!!! Why, he was sober. Everybody knows he was sober. He died of lung cancer!"

Oh, really?

And when did he go from a handful of cigarettes per day to a pack and a half? I see... it was *after* he quit drinking.

Good-natured Bob just swapped out one destructive behavior for another, and it took his life. It's the same with heart disease, stroke, and many other ailments.

"No, no, no– you've got it all wrong, Shelly!" says another. "Pat's diabetes and high blood pressure are what claimed her life."

Yes, that's true. And when did her problems with food begin? When did she gain eighty-five pounds?

I see, it was right after she quit smoking.

And her smoking?

Well, that became an issue after she quit drinking.

In other words, Pat replaced her addiction to alcohol and cigarettes with an equally deadly addiction to food. The real truth is that all three addictions eventually killed her.

But at least all her friends can take comfort in the thought that she died sober. She is no longer drunk, but she's every bit as dead. And she won't be coming to dinner anymore.

So sad, and so unnecessary.

We need to understand that when a hidden addiction is not handled at its root, it's still there, and it *will* be back– often with a vengeance. But, more importantly, when this occurs, missteps and mistakes made by those who mean well could ruin everything.

To be sure, for our loved one, they could be the last mistakes we make. So how do we plan to handle that as family and friends? What is the proper response, and what are the potential pitfalls? And can we count on getting anything of use from our governmental agencies, public or private institutions, or places of worship?

The answers are straight ahead.

Part II:
Passing By

"But when he saw the man lying there, he crossed to the other side of the road and passed him by."

Chapter 3

*　　*　　*

Menace To Society

Ronnie is an addict.

Speaking in slurs and half-truths on Denver's 16th Street Mall, he tells of growing up in the Midwest, the son of a housewife and a Navy Commander, a man whom he says he's only rarely seen.

Went to a private school, married the Homecoming Queen, graduated from a college he can't remember in a city he's never been, and then went to work on a top secret government project as a nuclear scientist.

Nuclear scientist?

Yup– that's what he says, anyway. As he tells it, the pressure was just too much, the people too fake, and the work too unrewarding. He needed to get back to where the real world lived.

Back to the street.

Chronically homeless, practically helpless, and in-between fixes, totally hopeless. As we spoke, the stench was beyond belief.

Overpowering.

Ronnie laughed with feigned bravado as he introduced me to his friends. J.J., the former pro ball player, Billy, the former star defense lawyer, and Jackie, the former supermodel, now six months pregnant with the baby of a man she says was "nice" to her awhile back.

His name? Well, that was impossible to know. As impossible, in fact, as sorting out the truth of their stories or the details of their pasts. As difficult as predicting the likelihood of any of them living to see another Monday morning sunrise.

As I speak with them, there are glimpses of the people they used to be, though fleeting, to be sure. Representative of the hundreds of others on the street this day, they can be at once both charming and incoherent, capable of arousing sympathy or profound fear. They understand and work the city's ordinances regarding panhandling, they claim to love Jesus... and given the right opportunity, any one of them could be extremely violent.

Yes, they are addicts. They are someone's sons and daughters, and they are victims, suffering from the devastating effects of a disease that long ago rendered them without control.

Only a fool would claim that Ronnie and the hundreds of thousands of addicted homeless don't present a societal problem, but let me be clear– they are are not *the* problem.

Addiction, not the addict, is the menace to society.

Meet William.

William is an addict.

From his cell at the State Prison, he marks his time. With good behavior and credit for the time already served, he should be out in another 1767 days. Without treatment, however, he will likely be back in for ten years to life within twenty-four months or so.

It is an old and familiar story, a painful and crushing tale, with explosive and terrifying consequences.

Early on, he was a bright young man who excelled at sports. Who can forget the passion, the energy, and the excitement of three undefeated seasons, or the interviews, the trophies, and the hype that followed?

But the real attraction was deeper.

With boyish good looks and a disarming combination of

intelligence, charm, and wit, William was a favorite of both teachers and classmates who voted him "Mr. Personality" and the guy who was "Most Likely To Succeed."

Scholarship offers flowed in.

Yale, Harvard, Stanford, and Columbia. The best law schools in the country. Presidents, senators, and the nation's top business leaders attend these institutions. Partnerships, recognition, and status were all on the horizon.

A marriage and three beautiful children followed, and then something went wrong. Very, very wrong.

Accusations of physical and verbal abuse, excessive drinking, pornography and gambling, unexplained financial loss and secretive behavior. When details surfaced of an affair at the law firm, his marriage came to an end.

Four months later, in what would be his brother's final ride, he fell asleep while driving home from a birthday party at his mother's house... drunk, with three passengers in the car.

From the State Bar to the State Penitentiary.

Addiction is a menace to society.

Surrounded by a whirlwind of laughter and activity in her congregation's Fellowship Hall, Mildred is at home. Since losing her husband, Gerald, to a heart attack last summer, she has thrown herself into a frenzy of volunteerism with a passion.

Need to coordinate that anniversary gathering? Decorate for the festival season? Organize the Ladies Guild or kitchen crew?

Mildred is good.

She's better than good.

She's creative, she's caring, she's kind, compassionate and competent.

And Mildred is an addict.

Though she doesn't know it yet, she won't survive the next two weeks.

Her claim to fame is baking, having worked almost two decades for Mauston Hill Candies. When the company closed in the mid-eighties, she brought her specialty home, and her creations have become a favorite of children and adults alike, especially around the holidays.

On this morning, "Grandma Sweets," as she is fondly known, is relating her concerns about an upcoming surgery. Diagnosed seventeen years ago with diabetes, she now is scheduled to undergo a gastroplasty procedure next Thursday.

The operation will go well– the recovery won't.

But at least now Mildred is among her best friends, and looking in from the outside, maybe that is what is so troubling. You see, there are four things that bond this dedicated group of women.

First, each possesses a servant's heart, and a desire to do good works.

Second, each of Mildred's friends are either significantly overweight or obese.

Third, each has been on one "diet" or another for as long as anyone cares to remember.

And fourth, not one in the group has any inkling of how to get to a real and lasting solution for the health challenges that they all face.

"Maybe if your surgery goes well, Mildred, the rest of us will all join you."

Unfortunately, Mildred won't be coming home this time, and yes, the others will join her soon enough.

These women are not the problem.

But their food addiction is a menace to society.

A NATIONAL DEBATE

In the previous chapter, I made the assertion that I believe that virtually *every* illness that we treat in this country is rooted, to one degree or another, in the disease of addiction. And you don't need to pay good money for me to write a book to convince you it is so.

We have already established that those suffering from addiction would like to quit, if only they could. Their inability to stop, in light of the known dangers, is indicative that addiction, in fact, is present.

And we know that addiction to various substances, activities, and behaviors results in specific and predictable illnesses and consequences that take their toll on the individual's health.

While aberrations may exist, illnesses such as heart disease, cancer, stroke, high blood pressure, diabetes, and the like are nothing more than *side effects* or *symptoms* of underlying and often hidden addictions to alcohol, prescription and non-prescription drugs, food, sex, gambling, tobacco, shopping, pornography, and more.

The long-term damage caused by the physical, mental, and emotional stress on the human body and mind lowers the natural resistances of the immune system and allows the destruction to occur.

Years of substance abuse, of unhealthy chemicals or modified genetic processes in our food, of secretive and deceitful behaviors, ultimately manifest in the disrupted health of our bodies.

Maybe it's just me, but the cost to our families and the burden to our economy should seem to make this issue a priority in any serious discussion or debate that is focused on resolving both the budget and the health care challenges facing our country.

That said, it is important for you to understand that as much as *The Samaritan Solution* is not a religious book, it is also not a political book. It is, in fact, a book about health.

The health of a people, and the health of a nation.

The health of your loved ones and mine.

And so I am incredibly thankful to be writing at a time when health care has come to the forefront of the national debate. Now, just in case you think it unwise of me to tie this work to such a contemporary issue– that you're concerned that it might become dated and irrelevant material– fear not.

I believe this is going to be an issue for a very long time for two reasons. First, the trends are that America is becoming less healthy each year, and second, there is nothing in the current health care debate to reverse that.

"Oh, yes," you say, "I heard they're going to tax soda!"

Please... that is a tax increase, not a health policy.

And it won't work.

Need proof?

The cost of cigarettes has risen hundreds of percent over the past few decades, much of it through taxation. Advertising channels have been closed, stiff penalties and fines imposed on establishments who sell to minors.

And the result?

Hundreds of thousands of people die each year from smoking-related illnesses. Only one in fifteen who try to stop do so for at least one year. Far fewer quit for life. And those who are addicted have shown the willingness to spend whatever it takes to get their fix. An extra nine cents on a SuperGulp Soda isn't going to affect consumption one iota.

The same is true for every other type of addiction.

So let's talk about health– and health care.

And let's ask the question of where we can go for answers.

You see, as families and loved ones who are struggling with the hurtful and devastating effects of addiction and its related illness, we often turn to society for help and solutions.

Yet, as the current debate has shown, those who should be in the know– and who have the power and the resources– have the ability to miss the big picture altogether.

Thus, we have witnessed a national conversation about the quality of care suddenly degenerate into endless arguments about who will pay for what, for whom, and with what penalties.

Yes, penalties– a big stick.

And while many will want to point fingers at this political party or that, please understand that there is plenty of collaboration in a system that has produced breakthrough treatments, but few cures, for an increasingly unhealthy and sick nation.

So, before we look to others for answers to our loved one's condition, let's examine the prevailing view of our culture toward disease in general, toward addiction in particular, and toward treatment of mere *symptoms* instead of proper diagnosis of *causes*.

THE POLITICIANS

Regardless of which side of the political landscape you live on, no doubt you have plenty of questions as health care issues are debated in Congress.

Progressives and Liberals are concerned with whether any administration will ever make good on the dream of a "Public Option" for insurance coverage, widely seen as a way to get to their ultimate goal of a single-payer system in which the government is that single payer.

Conservatives, on the other hand, are skeptical of any program that appears to trudge incrementally into what they believe may become– you guessed it– a single-payer system, with the government being the single payer.

They are all missing the point.

Long after the dust settles from the current squabbles, the health of our nation's people, and the system that provides the care, will remain one of our top priorities.

The problem is that no one seems to know what to do.

Socrates once said that, "As for me, all I know is that I know nothing." Indeed, when dealing with a subject as complex as health care and as explosive as addiction, when lives and relationships and careers are on the line, that is not a bad thing to admit.

You may wonder why, having focused relentlessly on addiction recovery for over four decades, I am now taking up the health care debate. Simply stated, the same lack of knowledge that permeates the field of addiction is also rampant in every one of the health care arguments.

In my opinion– and this *is not* political– neither our current President nor his advisers, nor anyone on either side of the congressional aisle, knows that the real problem with our health care system– the true cost– is a direct result of our treating the symptoms, as opposed to the causes, of disease.

As I said, this is an identical problem to one that I have fought successfully for over forty years.

When we treat the *cause*, recovery occurs, and the costs associated with an otherwise endless cycle of treatment come to an end. In short, the patient gets better– how radical is that!

However, when we treat symptoms, the expenses go on forever, or at least until the person dies from an illness that was often completely treatable.

That is what happened with my wife. It is what is likely happening this very minute with someone you care about deeply. It is what is happening with millions of our fellow citizens, and it is what could bankrupt this great nation under a mountain of unnecessary medical bills and red tape.

And that is the choice we face in the field of addiction: treat the cause or treat the symptom.

The difference between the two approaches is staggering, and needs to be addressed in the current debate. The real issue is about *why* we need to spend a *trillion* dollars in the first place, not *who* should pay it.

If the politicians don't understand this most basic principle, it is not likely that you will receive valuable assistance from them in your quest to save the life of the person you love.

One point, please, to clarify.

Since the current dialogue is all about providing more funds to insure more people so that they get the proper care, I'm afraid you may be thinking that if you just had access to more financial resources, or better insurance, you could get the help you need.

But money does not equal proper care. Proper diagnosis and treatment equals proper care. Consider this:

When Michael Jackson was buried, with him went a dirty little secret. While fingers have since been pointed, rightly or wrongly, at his most recent Dr. Feelgood, no one sees the decades of missed diagnoses made by other physicians who attended to him.

No one made the connection to the food addiction that led to his anorexia, the disease that was the precursor to his drug use and eventual death.

Similarly, Elvis Presley had his Dr. Feelgoods also.

In fact, it is estimated that toward the end of his life, he was spending over a million dollars a year to get the "best" medical care.

Not one of his doctors correctly identified his food addiction, the condition that led to his obesity, his drug use, and his premature death.

I bring this up for two reasons.

First, you should know that Mr. Jackson's anorexia and Mr. Presley's obesity are opposite sides of the same coin, and each is just as deadly.

It was their food addiction that was the real cause of their deaths, having never been diagnosed and treated successfully. Instead, each received one pill after another in an attempt to pacify the symptoms of their disease... and we all know that when one symptom disappears, another quickly takes its place.

Second, all the money in the world cannot buy good medical advice or great health care if medical professionals are unable to correctly diagnose the cause of the problem.

And this is what the politicians miss– every single time.

If you or your loved one are being treated *only* for a side effect or symptom of an illness, it doesn't matter who is paying for it, or how much.

You see, right now– whether funded by their employers, their fellow taxpayers, or their life savings– millions of Americans are suffering and will die because they are being treated for the symptoms of disease, and not for the actual causes of the diseases that will ultimately kill them.

Well, then, if there is no understanding within the walls of Congress as to the role of addiction in the surging cost of health care– if there is no plan on either side of the table that gets to the real issue– to whom can we turn next?

Certainly, a logical choice might be to look within the medical community itself.

FIRST, DO NO HARM

As we discussed, while the arguments continue to revolve around just *who will be covered* for what, and *who will pay*, the public is being ravaged by illnesses such as Alzheimer's, heart disease, diabetes, stroke, and cancer.

With all our education, and all our affluence, and in spite of the billions of dollars spent on research studies, the incidence of obesity, high blood pressure, and inflated cholesterol levels have gone through the roof– symptoms of diseases that will claim the lives of their victims decades early.

So now I have a question.

Do you believe that your doctor is equipped to get at the causes of these common illnesses in general, and able to diagnose a hidden addiction in particular?

"Well, of course I do, Shelly. I mean, after all, she's a doctor!"

Alright, and now I am going to tell you that it is my personal belief that, *when it comes to addiction recovery,* many doctors and medical professionals have no idea what to do.

"Now wait, Shelly. How can you say a thing like that?"

Because the doctors and medical professionals– the same ones to whom you are going for advice– are being treated for the very same symptoms with the same prescriptions, and dying of the same illnesses, as those for which they are treating you.

So, you tell me. If they knew the cure, wouldn't they be using it themselves?

I ask these questions because, as a therapist and as an addiction counselor, I have been successfully treating the causes of disease, as opposed to the symptoms of disease, for over forty years.

For those of us who are involved in this work, we find it difficult to believe that the *solutions* to common diseases appear to be so elusive to so many highly intelligent and highly trained professionals.

And we wonder what factors are contributing to– and who is benefiting from– keeping the people in the dark, satisfied with a prescription that allows them to live with illness, as opposed to curing it.

That's right.

We have developed into a culture that is satisfied with living alongside disease instead of eradicating it.

We will delve heavily into this mystery as we look at Big Pharma's role in the continuance of addiction, illness, and disease, but for now I must just ask the question– how could that be?

Is it corruption, ignorance, or indifference?

After all, this is not rocket science, it is medical science. And I believe it is medical science gone wrong.

So what does this have to do with addiction?

Thankfully, everything!

Since the beginning, those who have suffered from addiction of all types have been misdiagnosed and mistreated by one medical professional after another, while their physical condition deteriorated further and further.

And, unfortunately, on more than one occasion I have personally witnessed patients who, at the very end of their life, were physically shipped off to a counselor like me, to ensure that the patient wouldn't die on the hospital's record.

Strong words, I know.

Here is what many in the health community do not understand: your loved ones, individuals suffering from a medical condition called addiction– a disease whose victims are known by various titles such as overeaters, substance abusers, gamblers, and alcoholics– are branded as irresponsible, troublemakers, even criminals.

Yet, the truth is that they are really dying slowly of neglect. And slow death is *very expensive.*

How *tremendous* that the same problem is at the core of the financial mess that our health care system is in! How *wonderful* that now the rest of the country, with the world watching, can debate the issue! And how *fabulous* that the parallel between addiction and the health care system at large can finally be exposed!

Yes, addiction is the menace behind our skyrocketing and budget-breaking health care system!

Now, I know over the years I've been accused of finding addiction under virtually every stone. And it's true– start turning over the rocks of any major disease and you'll often find addiction down there somewhere.

And the response to addiction is the same as the response that has led to the current financial crisis in our health care system.

The symptom is treated, and the disease allowed to continue.

It's very lucrative.

Medicating symptoms over the entire course of a person's lifetime is *big business.*

Just one drawback.

The patient remains ill, slowly dying over a period of years. But the cycle of medical visits and pharmaceutical drugs keeps that sector of the economy humming right along.

Don't believe me?

Spend your lunch hour tomorrow observing the business at your local medical center, and then let's talk.

Over the years, I've observed that the treatment of symptoms often resembles what is known in other industries as *job security*– it keeps the patient coming back with great regularity for ongoing follow-up and seemingly endless rounds of medication.

On the other hand, when we find the cause– and when we treat the cause– the illness goes away. And when the illness goes away, the financial rewards that are built into the health care system also go away.

And therein lies the dilemma. Does it make sense for the health care system to cut off its own revenue stream?

Now, don't get me wrong. Doctors and nurses are highly skilled and exceptionally trained. But unfortunately, all too often this training has focused on identifying a symptom to which the answer is another pill.

Just as unfortunately, most Americans are content with their medications. After all, they're just what the doctor ordered.

But not you. You're different. You're looking for a solution. So, here are some questions to which you may want to get some answers.

What is the cause of high blood pressure, obesity, or diabetes? If you're not sure, would you like to know? Has your doctor taught you how to eliminate those symptoms for good, or has he or she given you a prescription for a pharmaceutical medication?

Further, will the prescription cure the condition– as, for instance, how an antibiotic kills an infection– or will the prescription merely help manage the condition over the remainder of your life? When you see others who are being treated with the same regimen, are they overcoming their disease, or slowly succumbing to it?

And when you look at your loved one who is struggling with addiction, are they beating it, or are they...

I'm sorry. I already know.

"THE PRICE IS RIGHT"

I really do have a problem with that show.

No, this isn't a rant about how Bob Barker could never be replaced. And in fact, I really like the glitzy prizes, and the girls are quite pretty. But have you ever asked yourself what pays the bills on one of America's favorite game shows?

Commercial after commercial after commercial after commercial after commercial– it's the drug industry's playground.

"Ask your doctor if the little green-speckled, polka-dot pill is right for you," says the announcer in a soft, attractive voice.

From another, "I had never heard of this before, but when a friend asked me about Lumpuckeroo, I knew it was time to see my specialist!"

And then the piano music begins, along with a thirty-five second monologue by a cheerful voice reciting a list of possible life-ending side effects as long as your arm!

And the public eats it up. Literally.

Yes, we are a medicated nation.

Now, I understand there are many who say they want to solve the problem, though– when it comes to addiction– most lack the skills required to bring about real recovery.

In fact, many who would get involved might actually make the situation worse. When your loved one's health is at stake, a "little" knowledge can be dangerous.

Now I hope you're sitting down, because what I am about to say next is rather explosive.

Okay, you had your warning.

Maybe the reason we are not finding *cures* for common illnesses and addiction is because it is not in some best interests to do so. Maybe some simply don't want it done.

Excuse me?

Well, let's look at an example from history. Polio was first recognized as a disease in the United States in 1835, and as awareness increased, so did reports of its prevalence in our society.

By the early 1900's, the cases numbered in the tens of thousands. By the mid-1950's, they numbered in the hundreds of thousands. And a shocked nation pulled out all the stops to find a permanent cure.

Did you hear that? What sweet music– *a cure*.

Under FDR, a national research foundation was formed, coinciding with the founding of the March of Dimes. Public support poured in, and the budget to fight the cause of the disease– to *wipe out* the disease– ballooned from less than two million dollars in 1938 to more than 65 million dollars in 1955.

And then, an amazing thing happened. No, *two* amazing things happened.

First, just a few years after Jonas Salk got passionately involved, the *cure* for polio was found, and the disease was stamped out as the leading cause of death of our children. What once seemed impossible had just become the reality for everyone who has lived since.

But more amazing is the fact that this researcher had *eliminated* the disease at its root– and with it, he eliminated the need for the ongoing medical treatment of polio victims for life.

Yes, he eliminated a potentially massive personal and professional revenue stream.

So I wonder...

How is it possible that, so often, with all our technology and all our money and all our education and experience, we can no longer find *cures* for common diseases?

Why could we do it a generation or more ago, but not today?

Why do we medicate tens of millions of our fellow citizens to help them manage their cholesterol, their blood pressure, their diabetes, cancer, and heart disease, but can't seem to completely eliminate it from their lives?

In fact, the trends are that these diseases are on the rise, more pervasive now than ever.

Is it possible– now, please hear me– that those with the *ability* to find the cures are *unwilling* to part with the revenue?

Is it possible?

Now you see why I suggested you sit down.

So I ask again.

Are the potential cures really that far beyond the knowledge of today's researchers and medical teams? How is it that we can create lifetime treatment programs to pacify symptoms, but seldom identify the cause?

And I just can't stop thinking. Back in 1968, I was 183 pounds heavier than I am today. I was suffering from rheumatoid arthritis, was addicted to alcohol, drugs, food, and gambling, and was under the care of four teams of doctors who had given me only six months to live.

I was dying from my disease, and from the side effects of the nineteen prescriptions I was taking.

And I ask... why?

Why was I able to eliminate all of those prescriptions, and yet others are content to take them for the rest of their lives? Why was I able to recover completely from my illnesses– the same illnesses from which you and your loved ones are slowly dying today?

Why would anyone listen to the litany of dangers that

accompany virtually every pharmaceutical drug and not question whether there may possibly be a better way?

And why, as the pharmaceutical companies have gotten bigger and bigger, have our country's people gotten sicker and sicker?

In 2007, over 3.4 billion prescriptions were written in the United States. More accurately, the real number is 3,457,595,838– that is an incredibly profound statistic!

Some examples from that year:

Wisconsin had 67,271,331 prescriptions written; a state with 5,627,967 residents.

Missouri had 93,268,928 prescriptions written; a state with 5,911,605 residents.

Illinois had 151,518,983 prescriptions written; a state with 12,901,563 residents.

And these records from the Midwest mirror those nationally. On average, the equivalent of over 11 prescriptions are written each year for every man, woman, and child in the country!

The numbers are staggering... as are the costs.

So, with your permission, I'd like to offer a question or two that you should ask before trusting someone else to heal your family's hurt.

How often is the *first line* of treatment for *any* medical condition a pill or prescription of one kind or another? Answer: *almost always.*

How often do our pharmaceuticals treat the underlying cause, as opposed to a symptom, of a disease? Answer: *almost never.*

How often do pharmaceutical drugs create dangerous side

effects that damage a patient's kidneys, liver, or other organs? Answer: Google the name of your prescriptions, along with the words, *"side effects."*

Then you tell me.

And while we're at it, here's one more: what bigger menace exists to our health care system than a progressive series of diseases for which no one is looking for a cure?

UNIVERSAL INSURANCE

Mark Twain once noted that, "Nothing so needs reforming as other people's habits."

As the debate over health care continues, the effort to continuously shift the focus and blame gets stronger. Note the recent move to change the direction of the talks from reforming "health care" to reforming "health insurance."

Of course, this further removes from view what should be the main issue in the entire conversation– that of solving the nation's health care crisis by improving the health of its people, and eliminating the causes of the common diseases that are running rampant in our society.

As we have discussed, when those who have the resources, assets, and knowledge focus only on who will pay to maintain a program of living with disease– as opposed to eradicating the disease itself– they sentence our families to live mediocre and often painful lives with illnesses that are unnecessary.

And– no surprise here– with medical costs estimated to run into the trillions of dollars, such an approach now also threatens our nation's treasury and our children's future financial security.

The news networks seek to identify a villain in the health

care story, and have conveniently settled on the insurance industry as a believable culprit.

This is understandable, of course, since reporters have been responsible for circulating many of the "who should pay" and "who should be covered" arguments to begin with. And, after all, it is the insurance companies who decide to raise rates, put caps on coverage, and deny service for preexisting conditions or high risk applicants.

Oh yes, and don't forget that the insurance giants also have *huge* buildings and are unquestionably and obscenely profitable.

So, now that the national debate has begun to swing toward the insurance companies, am I advocating letting them off the hook?

Absolutely not– but for a different reason than you might expect.

My issue with the insurance companies is not tied to their desire to make money. In fact, I believe that by helping Americans to stay healthy, they could eliminate hundreds of millions of dollars in expenses and earn even more!

But years of poor management, horrendous corporate decision-making, a lack of accountability, and rules that promote sickness over health have wiped out incredible opportunities on their part to make positive impacts in our society.

It has always amazed me what the insurance companies would pay for– and what they wouldn't.

For example, many will not pay for the most effective treatments for alcoholism, substance abuse, or food addiction, but they will pay once the condition gets bad enough to cause liver damage, heart disease, diabetes, stroke, or cancer.

By now you understand that many of the most common illnesses and diseases are mere symptoms of the real cause: hidden addictions to alcohol, prescription and non-prescription drugs, smoking, gambling, sex and of course the biggest of them all– food.

I have watched for years as insurance plans deny programs that would lead to healthy lifestyles and disease prevention, while they pay for unnecessary medical procedures that inflict trauma on the patient's body, a lifetime of unnecessary prescription medications that cause a host of damaging side effects, or ineffective rehab programs that see the patient using again within days of release.

Yes, the entire health care system in America actually avoids the promotion of the health of its citizens, and you and your loved ones are left to pay the price, in terms of dollars, shortened lives, and relationships that are cutoff prematurely.

And that's just for the mainstream diseases. Addiction is a whole other matter. When seeking help for your loved one suffering from addiction, many big institutions– like the pious priest in our *Good Samaritan* story– simply pass by.

WORK IT OFF

Remember Mildred?

We introduced the two of you back at the beginning of the chapter.

Mildred was a food addict, and a very kind lady as well. And in this section, we need to camp out on this point for a few minutes, as we'll do again when we discuss our country's food industry.

This is so important.

You see, I mentioned earlier in the book that food addiction will affect the lives of 70% of Americans, but now I must confess that is only partially true. Indeed, it is much worse than that.

So, let me rephrase.

If you are reading this book, food addiction *will* affect your life– one way or another. Either you will succumb to its various manifestations, or others whom you know will. Those are the numbers– period.

At the very least, with two out of every three American adults either overweight or obese, you will spend a significant amount of time at various points in your life engaging in activities forced upon you by this disease.

It is at the root of much of our health care costs, and it is completely treatable.

So, here is my suggestion.

Give people the tools, information, and resources to become truly healthy, and the need for much of the medical services and pharmaceutical prescriptions will disappear, along with hundreds of billions of dollars in health care costs.

Sound simple?

It is. So why does everyone look past it?

Right now, I want to focus on the one player who should have a positive impact on the weight loss debate, though alas, they have missed the mark as well.

And I am speaking of the fitness industry.

You see, it's not that we don't want to be healthy or lose the weight, it's that we just don't know what to do. We don't know what the cause of our problem is, so we try "solutions" that are doomed from the start.

For example, each year millions of Americans make New Year's Resolutions, most of which revolve around health: getting in shape, losing weight, quitting smoking or drinking, eating healthier.

And most will fail.

Fifty million of our fellow citizens will sign up for gym memberships they will never use, or home workout programs that will gather dust within weeks.

And it gets worse.

While infomercial after infomercial and magazine cover after magazine cover touts the exercise route to fitness, any program that misses the cause of the excess weight or obesity will only further damage the individual who is suffering.

And if food addiction is present– as it is in most cases of obesity– the chance of an exercise-based solution is nonexistent.

In fact, strenuous exercise may only increase the craving for additional carbohydrates, which produce the chemical changes and increased insulin production that are at the heart of the problem.

America is obsessed with health, fitness, and weight loss to the tune of almost sixty billion dollars a year.

So then why are so many adults either overweight or obese? In fact, why are so many adolescents overweight or obese? And why can't they seem to kick it?

Why are illnesses related to excess weight and obesity such as heart disease, diabetes, high blood pressure, stroke and cancer rampant in our society, and the reason behind our ballooning trillion dollar health care system?

Quite simply, the fitness industry, like the rest of the players, profits from treating the symptoms of the problem, and not the cause.

Sound familiar?

The truth is that proper nutrition, and the elimination of addictive trigger foods, will lead to optimal weight composition– and significantly reduce the risk of illness or injury– when combined with even mild exercise such as walking, gardening, or even light house work.

But that program is not a money maker!

Gee...

It couldn't really be all about the money– could it?

TRUTH, JUSTICE, AND THE AMERICAN WAY

A while back I wrote an online article about health care in which I stated that, within our system, "There is plenty of money to go around. And that, of course, attracts the lawyers!"

And to be sure, our Justice System has two very profound effects on the lives of those struggling with addiction and its related health considerations.

Let's look at the most obvious one first.

The lawsuits that are waiting around the corner for every medical decision have resulted in a culture of malpractice avoidance and high specialization, with the patient being shipped from doctor to doctor for further testing and diagnosis.

This is quite expensive.

In effect, the medical community must build a case so that if and when something goes wrong, they can prove that they have done everything possible to avoid it.

After all, that many tests, and that many opinions, couldn't be wrong!

The focus becomes treating the symptom at hand with the most current drug available, rather than diagnosing and treating the cause of the illness and returning the patient to true health.

For example, the most commonly written prescriptions today are for the control of high blood pressure, high cholesterol, and high stress and anxiety. Remember, these are all characteristic symptoms of an underlying problem. They are likely *not* the problem itself.

And as we saw before, in the absence of getting to the cause, the prescription will be required to be consumed by the patient for the remainder of their life.

Quite expensive, indeed– and very unhealthy.

But there is another– and usually hidden– side to this conversation, and it's one that is seemingly missed by all the players in the debate. It's the fact that the criminal justice system often plays a role in furthering addiction and addictive behaviors.

I wish I had a dollar for every page in the telephone directory in which attorneys advertise to get alcoholics out of drunk driving cases, or keep addicts out of jail who have become petty criminals to support their addiction.

Indeed, untreated addictions and their associated behaviors are the reasons that many are incarcerated in the first place– it is certainly no secret that addiction will frequently lead toward criminal activity as a means to pay for it. It typically starts with small infractions, followed by assorted slaps on the wrist.

But, all too often, the wrist-slaps bring with them no treatment and no therapy. To give a using addict a second chance without treating the root cause is an invitation to go ahead and continue their behavior– a real recipe for disaster.

By the time that their actions *demand* long-term incarceration, the individual has typically lost all control over their addiction, and the slide accelerates.

And eventually, as we have seen, it will always lead to the devastation of one's health. Sooner or later, addiction to *any* substance, activity or behavior will trash the victim's body, and that has to be paid for– regardless of where they live. So even locking people away won't avoid the addiction-related costs that are part of the nation's health care problem.

Further, addiction runs rampant in our corrections system today. Rather than reform, the criminal justice and prison environment often assists the addict, and in many cases provides everything they are looking for: drugs, sex, power, porn, and a culture of self-destruction.

Yes, self-destruction. Addiction, after all, is a form of slow suicide, stealing first the hopes and dreams of both the individuals and their families and then ultimately claiming the addicts' lives.

Now there is one more thing that you must understand, especially if you've reached the end of your rope and feel that maybe the justice system is what is needed to bring about recovery for the one you love.

I was recently told by a prison official that the recidivism rate at their maximum security facility is over 85%.

Recidivism is kind of a funny word– I've always had trouble pronouncing it– but the consequences are anything but humorous.

According to one dictionary definition, recidivism refers to "the chronic tendency toward repetition of criminal or antisocial behavior patterns."

Now certainly, this is nothing new.

Without the proper help, relapse is always high among addicts. What's so troubling was that, here we were in a "correctional facility," and no one seemed to know what to do to *correct* what had obviously gone so wrong.

BIG MEDIA GONE BAD

So, quick question:

Have you ever heard anywhere that our health care system focuses on the treatment of symptoms instead of causes?

Yes? Thank God!

Because that's just the response I got when doing an eight part report online about this very topic.

Suddenly, after weeks, people just began to get it. One day it just started to sink in, and we began receiving tremendous feedback.

And if my argument is correct, then this is quite important, because I believe that the entire health care system could be run at 15 or 20% of its current cost if only the American people learned to live truly healthy and moderate lifestyles.

I know. It's a pretty radical theory, isn't it?

And I also think that we could eliminate the vast majority of the destructive behaviors, as well as the physical and emotional wreckage associated with addiction.

Wait, let me rephrase, because that is clearly not a strong enough statement.

I know without a shadow of a doubt that the confusion and misdiagnosis that leads to ongoing illness, lifetime prescriptions, and ever-increasing costs can be eliminated completely once we identify and treat the cause of disease.

Period.

In fact, that is the very reason that I am so passionate about this issue. For years I have seen what happens– or doesn't happen– when those suffering from addiction are misdiagnosed and either mistreated or untreated altogether.

Now, Believer, here is what you need to know: not only is this extremely costly, it is very often completely unnecessary.

So why hasn't the media spread the good news that recovery and complete healing is available? What is their role in this whole debate?

I simply can't believe that with all the intelligence and resources– with the understanding and brilliance and investigative talents of journalists worldwide– that they cannot see what is going on in the U.S. health care system in general, and in the field of addiction in particular.

Or maybe there is another set of factors at work.

Please accept a quick reminder that money makes the world go 'round, and then answer this: is it possible that those who have the most to gain from keeping people sick also have the most clout when it comes to the support of mainstream media?

Just ask yourself– when is the last time you saw advertising on television from politicians, doctors, drug companies, insurance firms, fitness programs, or lawyers?

If you said, "Two minutes ago," that would be the correct answer.

Yes, money does make the world go 'round. And it also pays the salaries of big media gurus– the same celebrities who unfortunately die from all the same diseases as John and Sally Smith. Illnesses that, in many cases, are completely avoidable or totally curable.

Oh, and there is one other lobby that is mighty powerful. One other industry that spends heavily on the airwaves. And it is associated with the number one addiction in our society.

Hungry for more?

LET ME SUPER-SIZE THAT FOR YOU!

So, what if I told you today that the solution to virtually the entire health care crisis– and yes, the answer to eliminating much of *all* disease in the country– lay within one industry, and one set of behaviors that are common amongst our people?

And what if your Aunt Millie's diabetes and Brother Jake's heart disease weren't sapping the energy out of every family member every moment of every day?

What if the holidays could be fun again?

I've spoken of it many times, and will continue to do so.

Earlier you were given the figure of two out of every three adults being overweight or obese. So now, let me put it another way.

That means about 200 million Americans are going to suffer from one weight-related malady after another, until death do us part. And they can't just quit, because they are addicted to the chemical cycle and interaction between their bloodstream and their brain.

So grab your calculator, and let's just see if our practice of issuing lifetime prescriptions to treat obesity's symptoms adds up to good fiscal sense.

On second thought, you can leave the calculator– it doesn't go that high.

According to Stanford Hospitals and Clinics, obesity is a major health risk and cause of:

* High blood pressure
* Stroke
* Diabetes
* Heart disease
* Osteoarthritis and joint replacements
* Sleep apnea and respiratory problems
* Cancer of the breast, colon, gallbladder, uterus, and prostate
* Elevated blood cholesterol, inflammation and clotting issues

Other studies cite a plethora of additional ailments, including liver and kidney disease. So let's get to the cause.

If obesity is at the root of many instances of these diseases, wouldn't it make sense to look even deeper to find the cause of obesity? Why are diet and weight loss consistently at the top of so many people's resolution lists, and why will so many people fail to stay "resolved?"

Well, let me ask you this: does it make sense that the food industry would take it upon themselves to teach consumers about the dangers of highly-processed food? Or that substances like sugar, flour, and wheat in our diets can trigger the pancreas to go into hyperdrive, overproducing insulin, causing blood-sugar levels to alternately spike and then crash?

Can we expect great advice and help from an industry that profits the more people eat? Will they tell us that they've designed additives that promote binge eating or drinking, and cause withdrawal symptoms similar to every other addiction?

You already know the answers. And, unfortunately, a food addict's fix is legally available in every grocery store, and at fast food establishments on every corner.

Now, please, this is not to say that the food industry is forcing the American public to eat unhealthy food. No, in fact, they are just giving a nation of addicts exactly what we want.

Our bodies crave sugar, and the companies merely provide it in every imaginable form. From corn syrup to aspartame, and dextrose to fructose, over ninety substances in our food react with our body to have the same effect as sugar, leading down the familiar road to excess weight and obesity.

And the food industry's powerful lobbying and marketing efforts insure that the problem won't be going away any time soon.

After all, the truth is that it's just good business.

Super-sized products
+ Super-sized people
= Super-sized profits

Unfortunately, it has also become a super-sized menace to our society as a whole, and to the health of those we care about most.

TURNING TO EACH OTHER

We live in a 911 culture.

We're connected to the point where we rarely have to deeply connect anymore at all.

Someone else can help. Surely, someone else *will* help.

The accident at the corner, the car with a flat tire, the man on the side of the road. We simply dial 911 and keep traveling. No need to pull over, no desire to slow down, no reason to stop.

Now, Believer, please hear what I am going to say.

It is time... to stop.

Stop.

Would you stop already?

You and I and hundreds of thousands– no, *millions*– of Americans are either suffering ourselves, or suffering along with someone else who is.

And we can't call the politicians– they don't understand. The doctors and nurses are doing exactly what they know to do, and they do it extraordinarily well. But addiction's symptoms are a moving target, and not easily diagnosed.

The Justice System has zero resources to deal with the progressive nature of addiction, and the pharmaceutical companies, insurance firms, fitness industry, media, and food producers ultimately serve their shareholders.

And as we've seen– they're pretty darn good at it.

And then there's you.

Your loved ones, whether they know it or not, are counting on you. Mine are counting on me.

And you need to know that this is a very decisive moment where some families make it, and others don't.

But I have faith in you– you're in the game.

You're searching for answers.

You're reading this book.

I want you to understand very clearly that you can do this.

There can be life again, but you must avoid the critical mistakes that so many make when everything seems to go from bad... to worse.

Chapter 4

*   *   *

My Brother's Keeper

"Oh my God! Please help me! Please help! Please!" On March 13, 1964, Catherine Genovese, 28, was attacked and murdered in the early morning hours, just feet from her apartment's doorway in the quiet neighborhood of Kew Gardens in Queens, New York.

The young woman, known to friends as "Kitty," would come to symbolize all that was wrong with America. In a scene that would stun a nation and challenge our sensibilities, Kitty's death would send shock waves around the world.

But it didn't start out that way.

For all its brutality, it was nevertheless a story that may have gone largely unnoticed outside this hardworking, middle-class neighborhood. After all, New York City had hundreds of murders that year, and this one was no different.

By every account, the attack occurred as a completely random act of violence against a victim who just happened to be at the wrong place at the wrong time.

It was all over so quickly. Surely, nothing could have been done– or so it first seemed. And had that been the whole truth, the story would have died the same night that she did.

However, fourteen days later, on March 27th, *The New York Times* published an article that rocked the civilized world. In it they detailed the initial assault, the ensuing struggle and Kitty's escape. According to the newspaper account, the attacker then fled the scene, only to return after ten minutes to continue his crimes of rape, robbery and finally murder.

But that was not all.

You see, the charges that held the attention of country were not those that were leveled at the perpetrator.

Quite to the contrary, the *Times* article would claim that the real story was about neither the victim nor the killer, but about thirty-eight of her neighbors whom they claimed stood by and watched as it happened over a period of more than half an hour.

Thirty-eight witnesses... thirty-two minutes.

Those thirty-two minutes would change how we saw ourselves forever. For, in that time, it was reported that not one witness called for help.

Coming right on the heels of the JFK assassination, the story hit the press and airwaves with an incredible impact, rocking the nation to its core, questioning our values, our humanity and our very soul.

There would be international outrage and disbelief.

Foreign leaders would caution their citizens regarding travel to the States, local law enforcement agencies would brace for a series of copycat crimes, and small-town America would increasingly view its big city neighbors with fear and suspicion.

The Ugly American, the political film starring Marlon Brando which was popularized one year earlier, would take on a whole new meaning. America, once the sanctuary and destination for a generation of hardworking and oppressed immigrants, had become an ugly place indeed– chaotic and lawless, where neither Presidents nor women nor children were safe.

Thirty-eight witnesses. Spectators, according to the papers.

The questions were overwhelming.

Why would so many people stand by and do nothing?

How could they live with themselves? Had people really become so cold that they no longer cared for the helpless and victimized among us? How could they ever look at themselves in the mirror again? And what would they tell their children?

What had become of our morals?

Indeed, what had become of America?

In the years since, much controversy has surrounded the *Times'* version of events, and in fact, the newspaper itself revisited the story on the fortieth anniversary of the tragedy.

Were the assumptions reliable? Had all the facts come out? Was this really just an open and shut case of a nation which had become too big, too numb, and too heartless to take care of the needs of the very citizens who were most vulnerable?

Or could there be other explanations?

With the passing of time, several other theories have been advanced, and as we will soon see, they have everything to do with Samaritans– and addiction.

The first theory to explain the inaction of the witnesses is based on a concept that is common with large group dynamics. The idea is that everyone thought *someone else* would do something. As chronicled by Malcolm Gladwell in his blockbuster book, *The Tipping Point*, the very fact that so many watched it happen may have led each witness to believe they didn't *have* to get involved. Surely, someone else would intervene.

A second explanation that emerged was that the witnesses thought that there was no hope, that there was nothing they could do– it was just too late. This argument makes the case that many thought Miss Genovese was mortally injured in the opening seconds of the attack, and that as it became apparent that they were wrong– as every subsequent minute dragged on– their initial inaction caused an overwhelming sense of guilt and shame, resulting in denial and even further inaction.

Yet a third approach suggests that no one truly realized the seriousness of the attack. Maybe it was just a fight, or a lover's quarrel. Maybe their eyes and ears were playing tricks on them. Maybe it really wasn't so bad after all. Known as *pluralistic ignorance*, this theory suggests that since none of the witnesses were treating this as an emergency, there must not have been one.

And besides, they rationalized, this was a place where people still slept with their doors unlocked. Everyone knew that really bad things didn't happen in their quiet, friendly neighborhood. Maybe somewhere else, but not here.

Whatever the truth, three things are certain:

1) No one helped Kitty when she needed it most,
2) She left behind a grieving family and many friends, and
3) Quite unnecessarily, her funeral came decades early.

The power of such a story, of course, is that it looks right through us, and makes each one of us answer a central question. Faced with a similar set of circumstances, what would we do?

Would we help?

Or would we look the other way?

Of course, our immediate reaction, quite predictably, is one of defiance and incredulity!

"Why, you've got a lot of nerve!"

"I can't believe you'd even ask such questions!"

"I would never stand around and watch somebody die!"

"Of course, I'd help! I'm certainly not like those... those... callous New Yorkers!"

And, of course, we *must* tell ourselves such things.

It's a matter of rationalization and self-preservation. Like those witnesses in Kew Gardens that fateful night, we can't stand to think of ourselves in such awful terms.

So let me change the context and rephrase, and then let's you and I get *really* real.

What have we done, and what are we doing right now, to help our brothers and sisters who are are being ravaged by addiction at this very moment?

I said, let's get real, because they are suffering as you read these very words. To be sure, it has been estimated that virtually everybody knows somebody who is dealing with the physical, emotional, and spiritual health complications of addiction.

Think you're different?

Okay. Take all the millions of alcoholics, and all those hooked on both prescribed and illicit drugs, take all those killing themselves by intentionally inhaling smoke laced with at least thirty-seven known cancer-causing chemicals, and add in the reams of people– yes, even those within your church or synagogue– who are secretly accessing pornography, or engaging in hidden gambling or other compulsive habits, and lay that on top of the nearly 70% of American adults who are self-destructing with weight related illnesses, and then...

You tell me.

Now, please understand, I am not pointing fingers. You must know that there was a time when I also *did not* know what to do– when I, too, was overwhelmed.

Yes, I have seen the destruction first hand, and I've been on both sides. I spent years engaged in every addiction mentioned above. You name it, I've done it. And I've since spent decades pulling people and families out of the spiral of death that surely comes if proper treatment is not available.

Now, listen to this.

In 1973, after becoming sober, I made a list of forty-eight friends that I felt I needed to reach. It was time to make amends, if possible.

One by one, I checked them off. One by one, there was nothing to be done. Forty-seven of them had died, having succumbed to various complications that came with their addictions to drugs, alcohol, or food.

I met the forty-eighth in his Manhattan office. Sickly and weak, he was half the man he used to be and had lost part of his leg to alcoholic diabetes. He would join the others within months.

Now this is critical to understand.

Many of these friends were people of means, real movers and shakers. They had it all: the fame, the fortune, the influence, the power.

They had terrific businesses and vacation homes and investments and real estate. They were surrounded by politicians and professionals, doctors and lawyers and financiers, sports stars and celebrities. And now they were gone. Victims of a disease they did not understand, a lifestyle in which they aided and abetted each other's demise.

And that is what is so sad.

As their addictions killed them, there were onlookers everywhere– friends, neighbors, coworkers, business associates, and relatives– who watched them die.

You see, addiction involves others, and it leaves a trail of brokenness. Sadly, as these forty-eight powerful people were slowly dying, no one called for help.

Of course, their funerals were spectacular, and oh, so well attended, but they were held decades early.

So, why would family members or friends stand by and watch their loved ones die from perfectly treatable addictions?

Is it possible– as the theory in *The Tipping Point* suggests– that they're all just waiting for someone else to do something? Surely, sooner or later, mom or dad, or the boss, police, preacher, rabbi, or judge will reach them. Yes, someday, *someone* will know what to do.

Or are they feeling guilty, shamed or embarrassed? They wish they'd acted sooner, but see no hope now. It's just too late. There's been too much destruction, too much pain. They may be angry, hurt, full of blame, or justification.

And then there are those codependents who will rationalize, excuse or enable the addiction. They will use their own form of *pluralistic ignorance* to argue that it's really not that bad. Everyone does it– Susie just needs to cut down a little. And on and on and on.

Whatever the reason, I'm sure that the funerals of your loved ones will be just as moving as those of mine. Unfortunately, they'll likely be just as untimely.

But does it need to be?

In forty years, I have never met an addict who could not recover, nor a family that could not be healed, if they get the right kind of help.

And in that simple sentence is the good news and the bad.

Yes, the lives and relationships torn apart by addiction can be repaired. I've seen it thousands of times. Now here is the caution: rarely can those friends and loved ones do it on their own, and mistakes made at the moment of crisis can have devastating and long-term effects.

So, stand up and take a deep breath. Get a little fresh air. And when you come back, we'll look at the most common and costly errors that families make when confronted by the truth of addiction.

IN ROYAL COMPANY

Every so often an event takes place that galvanizes the hearts and minds of people from across the world, and, for a brief moment, places us all on the same page. Unfortunately and all too often, however, the most spectacular of such episodes– those containing the highest emotion and greatest impact– are fraught with misfortune and misery, with trouble and tribulation.

Consider, for example, the wedding between Prince Charles and Lady Diana Spencer. A wonderful ceremony, filled with beauty, splendor, and the dreams of a nation. It was viewed by an estimated 750,000,000 people worldwide.

On the other hand, think of the death of Princess Diana, an event that literally stopped much of the world in its tracks. The heartache so thick, millions of people became physically ill in the aftermath of the story.

And her funeral?

Well that was watched by 2,500,000,000 people worldwide. Yes, that's 2.5 billion people– more than three times the number who originally viewed her wedding, and representing over half the people alive on planet Earth at the time.

So, what does that have to do with addiction?

Well, maybe everything.

Another star, and a different kind of royalty, please.

A similar pouring out of emotions occurred as details became clearer in the death of Michael Jackson, and an uncomfortable and disturbing story emerged on what appears to be a very dark side to the life of the "King of Pop."

Details of anorexia, prescription and non-prescription drug

abuse, and a physical decline that some said left him unable to perform ever again, not to mention the fifty concerts that were scheduled to begin at London's O2 Arena within just weeks of his death.

And, not surprisingly, this event sparked many conversations of the similarity between Mr. Jackson and yet another king thirty-two years earlier. I'm speaking, of course, of the "King of Rock and Roll," Elvis Presley.

In each case, there was an aging star making a comeback. As mentioned earlier, each had a Dr. Feelgood, and the biggest entourage of medical and personal assistants that money could buy.

And I'm sure that if you spoke with the physicians, they would tell you that they were just treating the illness, the pain, the trauma. They needed to administer the medications. How else could their patients go on stage? How else could they function?

Unfortunately, these doctors were treating the symptoms of drug addiction with more drugs. And they weren't addressing the underlying issues of food addiction– in Presley's case, obesity, and in Jackson's case, anorexia– at all.

The real sadness in each of these stories, however, is the fact that such an end was so unnecessary, and indeed, so preventable. Just like those in your neighborhood, your place of work or worship, or your family.

Indeed, addiction kills, but only if it's allowed to run its course.

Here is an absolute fact– addiction never exists without leaving evidence. Certainly there were people who were close to these "kings," people who had inside knowledge of the breakdown of the men and their amazing talents. People who did nothing.

Yes, sadly, with the rich and famous there are always those

who are only along for the financial ride. But let's not be distracted by the circumstances surrounding celebrity, for there is plenty of pain to go around, and plenty of mistakes that are made.

What if you or a loved one are living right now with addiction to food, to alcohol or drugs, or maybe to gambling, smoking, sex or pornography?

What now?

There are three areas where families and loved ones typically make critical errors:

1) They do the wrong things,
2) They do nothing, or
3) They enable the addiction and behavior to continue.

Now, here is what you must know: these are common responses made by almost every family in almost every addictive circumstance. And each is just as deadly.

WRONG RESPONSE

Of all the things you can do when it comes to addiction, doing the wrong thing may be the easiest, simply because there are just so many wrong things you can do.

You see, when confronted early on with the truth, most families and friends start off badly and never really recover. The very first error many make is that they don't get involved in recovery at the first sign of danger, leaving the disease to progress unchecked.

In fact, because the early signals are often so subtle, most don't know they're on the road to addiction to begin with.

Additionally, the first hints of addiction within the family are often met by the family's own form of *denial*. And by the time their loved one's problem *really* becomes a problem, well, it's now blown up to become everyone's problem. It's one big public mess.

And the emotional roller coaster has begun.

Embarrassment followed by *frustration* leading to *blame* and *guilt* and *shame*. Handled poorly, the damage done at this stage can be virtually irreparable, and the pain and distress way beyond the scope that most families can manage on their own.

It is far too explosive. Far too emotional.

The problem with addiction is that, unlike other disasters, it isn't an event for which people plan. There's no drill. You know– if there's a fire, we all do this, and meet over here; in the event of a tornado warning, we'll all do that, and meet over there.

With addiction, families are often blindsided. They are confused, and they don't know what to do.

So Dad goes to the library, Mom asks a friend, everyone searches the Internet, all for textbook solutions to unique and extraordinary challenges.

Finding none, they try to wrest back control, issuing ultimatums that are not enforced, arguing with and condemning the addict, drawing up sides.

Looking for a definition of a wrong response?

I just gave you several.

And as the relationships break down, the little influence the family may once have had is lost forever.

Bitterness replaces forgiveness, and confrontation and punishment become the plan. They ostracize and humiliate. Tough love, it's called– let 'em hit bottom. That's what the book said.

Bad move.

Very bad move.

BOTTOMLESS PIT

So, here's how it goes.

Jamie's fading fast. He's been on the decline for years, but the last six months have been markedly worse.

"What are you going to do to help him?" a friend asks.

"What can we do? We've talked to him 'til we're blue in the face. I think he just needs to hit bottom. He has to want to get help– and when he does, he knows we'll be there for him. We've always been there for him."

It's a conversation echoed daily in homes and businesses and houses of worship throughout the country. It sounds so logical, so reasonable. Certainly, any rational person would want to get help as soon as things get bad enough.

There's just one problem. Jamie isn't logical, and he's definitely not rational.

Jamie is an addict.

Regardless of the brand, addicts don't ask for help. They aren't looking to quit. They're too busy trying to stop the pain, and that means getting the next round of whatever fix they're using.

Left untreated, the progression will follow a similar pattern.

You need to know that when Nancy attempts to curb her shopping addiction, it can just as easily lead to death as it could have if she had begun with cocaine, like your coworker's son. Her path may just take a different route– say from shopping to smoking to alcohol to food and ultimately a stroke or some other serious complication.

So if you think it's bad now, be warned.

The bottom is very ugly.

"But Shelly, don't you know? I mean, everyone knows that

the addict has to hit bottom. It's the conventional wisdom."

Yes, and now I have something to tell you.

When it comes to the field of addiction, the "conventional wisdom" has resulted in a 3% recovery rate, and the deaths of millions of people from perfectly treatable and completely avoidable maladies.

And while I will acknowledge that the concept of "hitting bottom" has been around a long time, here's a dirty little secret– one that many professionals won't tell you.

Are you sitting down?

When we wait for someone to hit bottom, we take the responsibility off of ourselves, and place it onto the addict. After all, they're the ones who got themselves into this.

It's a great little trick that removes any liability from the family or the medical professional to step in and arrest this very difficult progression.

In effect, we simply blame the person who is suffering.

"Now wait a minute, Shelly. Am I to understand that you're saying the medical people are avoiding treatment, setting up a scenario where they can pass blame onto the patient... all because the specialists don't really know what to do next?"

Well, Believer, consider this line of reasoning, think it through, and then you tell me.

The *hitting bottom* approach holds that before the individual can get better, they will need to sink to the very depths of survival. While they are down there, they must come to recognize the damage that they've caused and take responsibility for the fruit of their actions and the mess they've made.

They must consider their lot in life, rethink their options and come humbly, penitently, back on their hands and knees to seek forgiveness and a second chance at a new life. Only then can they begin the long climb back.

Yes, at the very moment of their greatest hopelessness and despair, they will realize how much you love them and care about them, and they'll understand that help is just a phone call away.

Though wracked with hurt and shame and grief and anger, overwhelmed by temptation and fear, they will pull themselves up by their bootstraps, and find the inner strength to "just say no."

Really.

I have personally treated more than nine thousand patients and their families who would tell you that the chance of that happening is the same as a snowball's chance in, well... you know.

They would also like me to tell you that they have some premium property they'd love to sell you in the Florida Everglades.

You see, unfortunately, when it comes to addiction, just wishing for a great outcome will not make it so.

You need to know that there are many "bottoms" in the life of every addict, and just when you thought it couldn't get any worse, it does. The damage done at each stage takes a heavier and heavier toll on the individual's health, self-worth, and relationships.

So why on earth do so many wait until the hurt is so extraordinary and the pain so great?

Please hear what I am saying in the spirit in which it is offered and then give this book to your friend whose son is struggling. Get a few more copies as eBooks for your coworkers or the board members at church who don't know where to turn.

Tell them. They must know that the real bottom in addiction is the end of their loved one's life.

They must know that along the way, there is a point of no return, a point where too much damage has been done, where the best medical treatment can no longer aide recovery.

Yes, tell them the place that they're all waiting for– the

bottom– comes the day they bury their loved one in the ground.

And the professionals... well, how can we blame them? I mean, it's really quite unfortunate, but look how terrible Randall's condition was when they finally got involved.

So they learn to console. "I'm sorry, Mrs. Brown. You knew how bad he was; there was really nothing we could do."

The truth is that there was plenty that could have been done– six months ago, six years ago, sixteen years ago. But since no one knew what to do, everyone just waited.

It is important to understand that the individual struggling with addiction is actively engaged in slowly and methodically killing themselves.

This cannot be overstated! Your friends, your neighbors, your loved ones, *are killing themselves.*

Right now.

The untimely deaths caused by the complications of alcohol, drugs, and smoking, or the diseases associated with food addiction– obesity, bulimia, and anorexia– are often decades in the making.

If, at any time, your loved one was having a heart attack, or if he or she told you they were thinking of ending it all, how long would you wait for them to hit bottom?

The answer, of course, is that you wouldn't. Sensing trouble, good people– loving people– step in and save a life. *That* is what the Samaritan did, and it's what separated him from the others.

So, let me give you a new definition of hitting bottom.

The bottom *is not* the place where and when the addict magically comes to the realization that they need help.

On the contrary, the bottom is where and when *you* say it is– that enough is enough, and you are willing to do whatever is necessary to begin the process of recovery.

The bottom is when *you* reach out. It's when you become the Good Samaritan, and find help in leading and managing the process of recovery and intervention.

The bottom, if you want it, is today.

NO RESPONSE

So then, many families who are faced with addiction initially make the wrong response– how do some other families respond?

Well, first it's time for a little review.

According to what we've previously discovered, addiction to alcohol and drugs will impact our direct health costs by over a $250,000,000,000 in the next 52 weeks, and yet the solutions are not part of our national discussions.

Interesting.

Addiction to tobacco will kill 440,000 U.S. citizens and burden our economy to the tune of $92,000,000,000 in the coming 365 days.

I know that earlier in the book I gave you these same numbers in terms of billions or trillions of dollars, but I give them to you here with all the zeros to help make the point.

Addiction is *really* expensive.

But at the same time, it does provide a very significant and now relied-upon source of tax revenue, so we sell alcohol and cigarettes on every corner and downplay the numbers.

And just to recap further, we know that over 60% of American adults will gamble this year, and 70% of men between the ages of 18-34 will be involved with pornography in the next 30 days.

And if any of this is going on in your home or with someone you love, you are about to find out quickly that addictions to these activities can destroy your relationships and tear the family trust to shreds in no time.

And then, of course, we spoke about food.

Encompassing anorexia, bulimia, and obesity, over 140,000,000 adults in America will be affected. In fact, it is likely that you either know one, or are one. Do nothing, and these conditions will steal the life of the addict, and drag your family through such painful complications as high blood pressure, stroke, heart disease, diabetes and cancer.

Yes, addiction is running rampant throughout our society. And while it affects almost everyone on one level or another, still many families choose this second response, which is to not respond at all.

So I must warn you.

If you find yourself in this situation, before this is over you will learn that addiction will only stay buried so long. Sooner or later, it will manifest in a very big way– in your health, relationships, and finances.

So let's talk about that.

Earlier, we mentioned how easily families and loved ones could make critical errors by doing the wrong things at the wrong times. With so many choices and so much confusion, that is certainly understandable.

But what in heaven's name would cause a family to do nothing?

What could they possibly be thinking?

Imagine for a moment that your husband or wife, your son or daughter, goes to see the doctor. It seems they've got an infection that they just can't shake.

No one's worried, however. It all seems simple enough.

The doctor will perform a series of exams, draw and analyze some blood and urine, work up some labs.

It doesn't get much easier than that. Determine the cause, find out if it is viral or bacterial, and treat accordingly.

Right?

But what if that didn't happen?

What if instead, the physician said he wasn't going to do any tests at all.

"No, let's just wait and see," he reassures.

"Okay," you ask, "what exactly are we waiting for, and what do you expect we will see?"

"Well," he says, "It may not be as bad as it looks– if it's viral, it'll just go away in seven to ten days."

"And if it's bacterial?" you ask.

"Oh, well, in that case, it'll just continue to get worse and worse, and then, well... then he'll die. But at least we'll know for sure."

Excuse me? You wouldn't play such games with bronchitis or strep or pneumonia. Why would you play them with a disease as destructive as addiction?

Now, you can put this next statement in the bank.

Of all the mass uncertainty that surrounds living and loving in an addictive environment, one thing is absolutely indisputable: the "Do Nothing" strategy is a real loser.

So why then do so many families do nothing?

Good question. Here are the answers:

First, as we know, many people faced with the addiction of a friend or loved one initially respond with denial.

Second, based on their desire for status, popularity or the approval of others, they invite in a few of denial's friends, *shame* and *embarrassment*.

And third, considering their options, they have a heavy sense of *hopelessness*. Let's break each of these down.

Remember that denial is a response that admits the activity, but not the seriousness of the problem. Addicts use this all the time. In fact, it is one of the identifiers that addiction is actually present.

So we hear that, "I'm not really smoking that much," or "Yeah, I always put on a little weight this time of year," and many other seemingly innocent statements. But as we will see in the next chapter, denial that is pushed can become very aggressive.

So, we understand the addict's use of the denial tool, but here we see that, quite often, families and friends also use denial. So suddenly, when asked, we have Mom explaining that, "Richard just likes to blow off a little steam at the casino," and while he does seem to have really withdrawn from family, "at least he is with friends when he gambles."

Hmm... Richard's wife thinks differently.

Tired of staying home on weekends, she wonders what else might be going on during his now-frequent trips to Las Vegas. And she's right to be concerned because Richard's addiction is not confined to the slots and tables.

Further, other cracks are now beginning to show– the stress in the marriage has begun to manifest itself, with Richard's mother and Richard's wife on the verge of opening battle lines with each other and with sides being drawn.

Mom says it's no wonder her boy gambles, married to a woman like that. And besides, the boy's father gambled for a time also; this *is not* that bad. It is the picture of the ostrich with its head firmly buried in the sand, thinking this is not a problem. It is just a phase– it will go away.

And she could be right. If it *is* just a phase, it *will* go away. If it is addiction, however, it *will* get worse– eventually *much* worse.

As mentioned, the second reason that families do nothing is rooted in their own shame and embarrassment. This is truly sad, because it accomplishes nothing.

Now understand, shame is very different from denial. Unlike denial, which says that things aren't that bad and they will go away, shame says this is *really* bad and it also doesn't *look* very good. And they hope it goes away before anyone else sees it.

Now here is an important point.

Families who struggle with shame and embarrassment almost universally reject addiction as an illness. Instead, they view it as weakness, selfishness, or rebellion, and the addict as one to be brought into line and punished. Yes, they are embarrassed by their friend or family member. And they also tend to really resent their loved one's behavior.

Unfortunately, addiction that blossoms in this environment almost never ends well.

Finally, hopelessness accounts for the third reason that families or friends do nothing. Unlike denial or shame, hopelessness fully admits the severity of the addiction, and– at least for a time– is willing to let light shine in on the problem.

However, these are people who really believe that they have tried everything, and who usually *have* tried many of the wrong things, only to find themselves defeated, back at square one.

These are the families who engaged in tough love, who have spoken with counselors and medical professionals. They have tried and botched physical interventions, and torn each others' feelings to pieces.

They have been angry and frustrated. They've bought books and DVD's and self-help programs, they've paid for one rehab and then another.

And they've prayed. Oh, how they've prayed!

They've done everything they believe they could have done, and now they no longer believe there is anything that can be done. Hopelessness removes the glue that holds relationships together, leaving families and friends standing by in resignation, waiting for the end.

NO ONE HOME

There is one more set of circumstances that we must discuss before we move on– one more condition that is a reflection on our life and times.

Never before in the history of the world have we seen a breakup of the family unit and structure as we see in America today. And please, Believer, don't think you're immune.

As we know, Scripture plainly tells us that all of our afflictions "are common" to all mankind. That means sickness and depression and rebellion and addiction and temptation and adultery and divorce.

And with the breakup of the home, many parents aren't really all that involved with their children, in good times or bad. The family isn't there when illness and addiction occur because, well, the family is *never* really there. That's just how it is.

So, when Bobby hangs with the wrong crowd and gets involved with drugs and pornography, no one is there to notice. When Lisa cries out by cutting herself or engages in behavior that makes her a play toy at school, no one is available to care.

Known as *neglect*, Mom and Dad, aunts, uncles, cousins, pastors, priests, rabbis and teachers are all preoccupied, all too hurried. And like those in the parable of Jesus, they all pass by without stopping when they see trouble.

It is the purpose of *The Samaritan Solution*– and of my practice, for that matter– to change these factors forever.

If you are experiencing denial, shame, embarrassment, hopelessness, or neglect, I want you to know that you are not alone. And, as you will very soon see, complete recovery and restoration is possible.

AN ENABLER BY ANY OTHER NAME...

Okay, so let's level with one another.

Deep down, you know without a shadow of a doubt that there's a problem, and there's also no question as to what it is.

Addiction.

If you've read this far, you know that the substance or activity of choice matters little– left untreated, the spiral will continue, ultimately robbing your loved one of his or her health and vitality, and stealing years from your relationship together.

So what now?

Well, if you have a rational and ordered mind (and I trust that you do), then it is likely that you've already read the beginning of this chapter before you stumbled here.

And indeed, if you've done that, then you know that there are critical areas in which families and friends often make devastating mistakes when trying to deal with the addiction of a loved one.

You know that some of these errors will merely take you to a place of pain and misery, and others will show you just how much further down the bottom *really* is.

Quick recap. We discussed the fact that many families, when confronted by the overwhelming emotions connected with addiction, respond by doing the wrong things.

We recognize addictive environments are often dominated by emotions like embarrassment, frustration, blame, guilt, and shame. We understand powerful feelings of pain and distress characterize the explosive nature of relationships that are way beyond the scope that most families can manage on their own.

Further, ultimatums and arguments, bitterness and condemnation, punishment and humiliation become the norm, destroying both the bonds and the influence that families once may have had.

We then broke down the opposite side of the issue, those families and friends who do nothing at all.

These are folks who are often practicing their own form of denial, refusing to acknowledge the severity of their loved one's condition, passing it off as a phase.

And finally, we spoke of others who have fallen into a state of hopelessness. Having tried everything they can think of, and often many of the wrong things, they now resign themselves to a sad end that they consider to be inevitable.

And maybe through all of that you're feeling pretty good right now, thinking that whatever you have or haven't done, at least you didn't make those mistakes!

"Whew! Thank goodness for that!"

Well, not so fast.

You see there is a third category– and this one's a real killer.

Literally.

Known as *enablers,* these people have it all figured out. They believe they can keep the situation under control, and under the public radar. And they do so by rationalizing that they are actually helping the addict.

The forms this can take are as diverse as the people involved, but it typically involves activities that provide cover.

This could include doing things for the other person that they should be doing for themselves, arranging both schedules and the environment to accommodate the addictive behavior, making excuses to justify improper activities, and the like.

Enablers walk the finest of lines, engaging in behaviors that they know to be wrong, all the while justifying that their actions are done for the right reasons. So, when Jeannie calls into work for Robert saying that he came home feeling quite ill last night and she's worried about the Orangutan Flu, she must now somehow rationalize her actions.

Yes, Robert *did* come home from the bar feeling ill last night, and yes, the whole world is worried about the flu, but that *is not* why Robert is still in bed this morning, and Jeannie knows it.

Truth is always one of the very first casualties of addiction.

Enabling, then, does three things:

1) It *empowers the addict*, making them bolder in the belief that they can get away with their behavior,

2) It *hurts the addict*, by allowing the destructive behaviors and activities to continue unabated, and

3) It *hurts the enabler*, by compromising their integrity and forcing them to continue to live in an addictive and often dangerous environment.

So why would a family member or friend knowingly or willing hurt their loved one? Answer: they wouldn't. So why do so many live a life of co-dependence and not seek proper help?

The answer is that most don't know that real help exists, that solutions are available. The average American's view of addiction recovery is what they see on the entertainment shows or reality TV.

These cases, as we so frequently witness, tend to be absolute train-wrecks. And the more we see, the more it appears that the abnormal is normal. It's no use, they think– nothing works anyway.

Enabling kills. Shortly after the death of Michael Jackson, his sister LaToya was quoted as saying that she now believes her brother was murdered for his money– that those who *should* have had his best interests *didn't*.

And, of course, at the very least, the second half of her statement is correct.

However, it is likely that there are far more accomplices than she or anyone in the family will care to acknowledge. Now please, with all due respect, don't be distracted by the fame, the celebrity, the 24/7 coverage, or the lavish memorial displays.

The same practices that enabled the star's addictions to continue are also at work today in our own families and neighborhoods, and in our places of work and worship. These are the true enemies we face as we work toward the recovery of our loved ones and ourselves.

Most importantly, you must prepare for the fact that addiction is most often very raw, almost always volatile, and potentially intensely harmful to everyone involved.

It is not the environment to make mistakes, no place to give this idea or that idea "a try." Indeed, addiction is a place where your next error can be your last.

It is a place where you will need *The Samaritan Solution*.

Part III:
The Samaritan Solution

"... and when he saw the man,
he felt compassion for him."

Chapter 5

*   *   *

Everyday Heroes

He was certainly nothing to look at. Real heroes seldom are. In fact, in the glitz of our big media and celebrity-driven culture, he may not have even been noticed at all. But deep down, you and I both know that these are the stories we like to hear. These are the tales we love to tell.

Yes, they are the adventures that warm our hearts, and the narratives that fill us with hope and inspiration and vision for the future.

We want to read about the loyal canine who rescued a sleeping family from a home on fire. Oh, please tell us about the off-duty nurse who recognized *America's Most Wanted.* And can you believe the 91 year old great-grandmother who lifted the 3/4-ton pickup, freeing her neighbor who was pinned underneath!

Well, actually, I must admit I've always had trouble believing that one.

Ahh... but I digress.

The point is that *Everyday Heroes* are the real deal!

Far from the stage and screen, hidden from the limelight, out of the public eye and removed from the television newscasts, these are the people who make our nation great and return the confidence that, even in the darkest of days, life can be good again.

And here is, perhaps, the biggest attraction.

You or I may never invent the next great technology or perfect a revolutionary new medical procedure. Nor may we win the

Super Bowl or produce the next hit movie. True, we may not travel to distant lands and bring water and agriculture to starving children, but, hear this loud and clear– you and I can save a life today!

You see, the greatest thing about recognizing an everyday hero is that tomorrow you may be one of them. But here is the caveat:

You *may* be one, but *only* if you are willing.

THE POWER OF THE WILLING

So, what is it about the parable of *The Good Samaritan* that allows it to stand the test of time? Why has it been repeated throughout generation after generation, and why is it that this story could be told with slight variation in any culture on the planet?

The answer is simple: everyone gets it.

From the villages along Vietnam's Mekong River Delta to the Outback Down Under, from the coal mines of Northern China to the fashion capitals of Milan and Paris, from West Africa's Ivory Coast to Europe's Ivory Towers, they all get it.

But don't be fooled. Just because it is easy to understand doesn't mean it is easy to follow. No, on the contrary, with all the cares and concerns of modern-day life, between juggling careers and kids and finances and family responsibilities, our desire to stop and engage with someone in need can be in extremely short supply.

When stacked against the daily "to-do" and "to-spend" lists, the demands on both our calendars and checkbooks can easily seem to outweigh our current willingness to help others, to evaluate options, to search for solutions and to pay a substantial price, if necessary.

But those who do become today's heroes.

Yes, those who are willing.

The question for you, of course, is the same as it is for me.

Are we willing to pay the price to become an everyday hero in the life of our neighbor? Will we give our time and attention, our focus and energy and love, to help an addict get the treatment required to save their life?

Here's another one: will we give our money?

Ouch.

"Now c'mon, Shelly, that's hitting below the belt– why do you always have to do that? You don't know how tight things are right now, what with a job change, and Sally's mum is moving in with us, you know, and the twins– well, the twins are about to graduate high school, and head off to..."

"Besides, Shelly, we've tried and tried with Billy, and he just doesn't listen! It's constant with him! I really believe he just needs... to... hit... bottommmm... oh, shoot."

By Jove, I think you've got it!

So let me rephrase in the clearest terms possible.

In spite of your career move, and notwithstanding the mother-in-law– forgetting for a moment that the *obedient* kids will soon be taking their SAT's– yes, putting behind you all of the failed attempts to bring Billy back into the fold, are you still willing to look at treatments to help your *troubled* son, before you need to bury him? And while we're at it, are you willing to do the same for someone else's son?

I'm sorry– that's not hitting below the belt.

That's loving your neighbor.

You see, the Good Samaritan was an everyday hero.

That said, I believe it is helpful for our conversation as it relates to addiction, and as it relates to your friend or loved one's illness, to examine just what it was that made this Samaritan "good."

Was it his quick thinking?

Was it bravery?

Was it his knowledge of first aid?

Indeed, was this man a physician?

Does the story itself lead us to believe that he was highly trained, or that he possessed a range of special qualifications to do what he did?

Right to the point– was he *good* because of *what he did?*

I don't think so.

I believe he was *good* because of *how he loved.*

His *goodness* is directly related to his *compassion* and his *willingness* to act to help his neighbor– even one who hated him.

I don't believe it is a stretch to claim that had Jesus put this character into any other context, our man would have responded in a very similar and predictable manner.

Yes, he would have heard the dog barking and rushed into the burning house. He would have been the nurse who called the local sheriff. He would have been the great-grandmother hoisting the truck off of her...

Okay, so I still have trouble with that one.

But the Samaritan was *good*, simply and for no other reason than that he saw trouble and was *willing* to get involved.

Don't believe me? Ask yourself this.

Had the man died, would the Samaritan still have been good?

Of course.

In other words, his willingness to help preceded the situation in which the help was needed. So, when danger arose, the decision to get involved had already been made.

He didn't have to think about it.

No time was required to be spent mulling over the pros and cons, and he didn't have to evaluate whether the victim was worthy of his sacrifice. That decision, too, had already been made.

The victim, like himself, was a child of God. Similar, I suspect, to the addict in your life or mine.

Now let's leave our first-century discussion for just a minute, because this is so important.

Often, when working in the field of addiction– when things start to get really raw– there are three times when well-meaning and otherwise caring people– yes, even very spiritual or highly religious individuals– turn their backs on their fellow man, literally leaving them to die.

The first is when we begin to feel that the addict really deserves what they have gotten, believing that through the recklessness of their own behavior, they've brought it all on themselves. This belief is rooted in a warped sense of justice.

The second occurs when we conclude that a friend or loved one has gone past the point of no return, and there is just nothing else that can be done. This belief grows out of hopelessness.

The third and most destructive is when we believe that issues in other peoples lives have no effect on our own– in effect, we have nothing to gain or lose in the transaction by bringing aid to a distant acquaintance or stranger. This belief is born out of selfishness.

And as we shall soon see, Jesus offered a special warning on this final point to those who would hold themselves up as examples of Godly living.

Indeed, The Word is replete with expectations that we will not only learn the principles by which to live, but that we must also apply them.

Pick up any version of the Old Testament Scriptures and you

won't get far before you hear the question, "Am I my brother's keeper?" Of course, this was also the title of our last chapter here in *The Samaritan Solution,* and it is quite applicable to those of us living with addiction. For convenience, I'll summarize it here, and you can find it for yourself sometime in *Genesis 4.*

Check out the whole story for the context, but let's just say that those five words– which have also transcended all recorded history– were asked very sarcastically by a man named Cain just after he had caused the death of his brother, Abel, and right before the Lord spanked him for all the world to see.

Since that time, believers everywhere have come to view this phrase in a slightly different context. Even a loose understanding of Biblical principles would seem to shout from the pages with exclamation, "Yes, indeed! You are absolutely and most definitely your brother's keeper!"

Throughout the Old and New Covenants we are also commanded to take care of our parents and grandparents, our spouses and children, as well as the poor, the needy, the sick, the elderly and the widows.

Oh– and lest I forget, our enemies.

"Now, just wait another minute, Shelly! I agree that I'm responsible for my family, of course, and my friends, maybe. But I certainly don't have time to care for the whole world– and, to be honest, there are some people that I really don't want to help, either! Enemies? C'mon, get real."

I understand.

No, let me be more exact: I understand, completely.

And I'd like to make several points.

First of all, we've definitely made some headway, and I appreciate your honesty. The fact that, as believers, we can come to a point where we admit that we're really not interested in helping some people is a major leap forward for most of us.

Second, your admission of responsibility to help those in your sphere of influence to recover from addiction is likewise a giant step in the right direction. Please know that before this book is finished, I will likely hold you to your commitment to helping your loved ones, and will offer to walk the road with you.

For now, though, let me just remind you that the whole "loving your neighbors and enemies" thing wasn't my idea.

But it is the expectation that was laid out for us.

You see, when Jesus set up this story, He knew exactly to whom He was speaking, *and* how they would take it. Further, He wasn't one to waste His words. If a concept was in there, it was likely in there for a reason.

A quick recap of history may be helpful.

The ministry of Jesus Christ was focused initially on the Jewish community of the time, and based out of a city on the northern shore of the Sea of Galilee called Capernaum.

All of His early converts were Jewish, as were His most trusted and hand-picked disciples.

In fact, Matthew records that, *"Jesus sent out the twelve apostles with these instructions: 'Don't go to the Gentiles or the Samaritans, but only to the people of Israel– God's lost sheep.'"*

Which, by the way, likely irked the Jewish leadership, who absolutely *did not* consider themselves to be lost!

Now rewind to about a thousand years earlier. The unity that had been achieved by King David, and the peace and prosperity that had flourished under his son, King Solomon, was shattered when Solomon's son Rehoboam took the reins from his father.

In case you think this has little relevance to life today, let me tell you that it was the issue of *high taxation* that led to a rebellion that broke the country in two– the Northern Kingdom and the Southern Kingdom.

Fast-forward three centuries. The year is 722 B.C., and the North's capital city, Samaria, is barely holding up under a three-year siege by a contingent of Assyrian warriors who were eating up real estate with a vengeance from their home base in and around modern-day Iraq.

The following year, it would fall to King Sardon II, who would burn Samaria to the ground and cart off its twenty-five thousand residents into slavery.

In their place, foreigners and refugees would be relocated into a rebuilt city and would intermingle with the handful of Hebrews that remained, creating– you guessed it– a group of despised and rejected half-breeds called Samaritans.

Considered pagan and unclean, one would never willingly associate with a member of this contaminated sect.

Yet, this is the group that Jesus would use to teach and admonish the Jewish leaders and his own followers about such principles as hospitality, thankfulness, and compassion.

Yes, it was at Jacob's Well that Jesus ministered to a Samaritan woman, actually drinking from her cup in a display that rocked his followers. And Scripture tells us that her testimony led many to believe– quite a shock to the Jews who had dismissed His ministry.

And later, when Jesus healed ten lepers of their disease, only one, a Samaritan, returned to thank Him for what He had done.

And now this.

A story in which a Jewish man is beaten, robbed, and left for dead. And not one, but two religious leaders pass by their helpless, dying brother– and a Samaritan provides the necessary love, care, and compassion that becomes the stuff of legend.

How ridiculous!

But the point was not to irritate. The point was to instruct.

And before anyone gets on their high horse to ridicule the Jews, I have a question that I must ask you now. And let's get very serious for a few minutes here.

If I came into your life, and lived with you for two weeks– if I met your friends, your spouse, your children, and extended relatives, if you introduced me to your coworkers and the members of your church or synagogue, and I hung out with you at the common places that you shop and have friendly acquaintances and relationships– yes, if we did all that, would I meet any addicts who are slowly self destructing?

Addicts whom you've been passing by?

I'm sorry, but the numbers suggest that it is so.

Now, please, we've come far enough together in this book for you to know my heart. And maybe you've also spent some time on the web researching some of the tools we've made available there.

Or maybe you've downloaded or listened to various multimedia talks or heard me speak publicly at a seminar or conference.

If so, you know that this is not about you, and it is certainly not about me. It's not about blame or intimidation or pointing fingers.

This about helping our brothers and sisters who are dying, and about equipping you right now to be the everyday hero that I know you want to be– the everyday hero whom your loved one *needs* you to be.

And that is all that matters.

COMPASSIONATE LEADERS

What was I to do?

More to the point, what was I to do *now?*

Thirty-four years of my life had just come and gone with the swiftness of the Nor'easters that Maureen and I had weathered so often throughout our time together.

And now she was gone.

The food addiction that caused her cancer and slowly eroded her body had also taken its toll on me. The pain inflicted by this disease is destructive on so many levels. Hers had dragged on for seven long years, and culminated in stealing this beautiful woman's life when she was just fifty-four.

Oh, how I wish I'd known earlier what I know today.

Oh, how badly I want you to know now.

The questions raced through my mind– how can I make the biggest impact? Who is willing to listen? With obesity on the rise in every demographic, why isn't the word getting out?

Why don't people know the cause?

More importantly, why don't they know the solution?

That's it– that's it, I thought!

What this disease needs is a foundation, a foundation that is dedicated to eradicating addiction's influence and destruction from our nation's families!

What's needed is a light to be shown in the darkness, to bring an awareness of the treatments available, treatments that could save the lives of all the other "Maureens" out there! What's needed is someone to speak to the victims and also for them!

What's needed is a team of missionaries on a new kind of mission. Yes, an entire army made up of a different type of warrior–

Good Samaritans, who are willing to learn and grow, and then share and go.

What was needed... was me.

And I believe that there's a strong chance that, before you are through reading this book, you'll know that what is needed– is you.

The year was 2005. I settled into a new home in a new community with a new plan. If I was going to be a missionary, the logical place to begin, I figured, would be in the churches or synagogues.

So to church and Temple I went.

I knew I'd be welcomed with open arms!

After all, the numbers of kind, wonderful, loving, and compassionate people who are dying slow deaths from addiction are the same within the nation's churches as they are without.

Obesity?

Yup, just as prevalent. Don't believe me?

Look around for yourself at your next weekend service or potluck banquet. I believe you will find that the percentages of overweight members in your house of worship will mirror the two out of three that exists for adults across the country.

What about illnesses such as heart disease, cancer, stroke, high blood pressure and diabetes?

Uh-huh. All the same.

The use of tobacco, alcohol, gambling and pornography? Or the rates of divorce, depression, adultery and suicide? They may be hidden, but when the surveys are confidential– when secrecy is assured– the results are always the same.

The same issues that plague the secular world are at work in the lives of struggling believers also.

As you know, that is Scriptural.

So imagine my surprise as I met with pastor after pastor after priest after priest after rabbi after rabbi, and all showed me the door! Well, actually, they didn't show me the door, they just asked that I not speak with *anyone* about addiction once I came through it.

One by one by one by one by one by one... forty-two houses of worship in all, maybe sixty or seventy church leaders, all either consciously or unconsciously *passing by* their sickest, most fragile, and vulnerable members.

Why would they do that?

And what would Jesus say to them?

Why is it okay to allow our friends and family members, our coworkers and fellow congregants, to be systematically rendered helpless by diseases that could be treated much more effectively– or, better yet, avoided all together?

Why do we wait until they are so sick, or their relationships so damaged, before we get involved or lend support?

And why do we shun any discussion of addiction, while we embrace the diseases that are often the very *evidence* of addiction's presence in the life of our neighbor?

Why can't we talk about the cause?

To clarify, suppose for a moment that an upstanding member of your church had a loved one that was diagnosed with a treatable form of cancer.

But here's where things go wrong.

Instead of investigating the most effective form of treatment, searching for the best oncologist, and evaluating all of the options, they turn around and brand that family member as a black sheep. Everyone cuts him off.

Yes, they get frustrated with him– then angry.

They begin to lash out!

"Just *quit it* with that tumor already!" they demand.

Next the congregation gets in on the act. The pastor and the elders think that it might just be better if this person goes away. After all, he's not very pleasant to be around, and he seems to be increasingly more trouble.

What would you think of that family and that church body for ostracizing their loved one at a such critical moment?

It's ridiculous, isn't it? But it happens every day with countless people who don't understand the medical realities of addiction– people who are embarrassed and ashamed and who just don't know that there are solutions that really work!

These families suffer in silence.

They hope, they pray, and when the answer knocks on the door, they say, "Shhh... we don't want anyone to see us like this!"

Well, the message of this book is that it's okay to come into the light. No, it's *necessary* to come into the light. I want you to know that there is life after addiction, and you may have it abundantly.

THE OTHER SIDE OF WILLING

So, by now you must be wondering– out of the scores of clergy with whom I met, how many have been willing to actively promote the beautiful message of hope and recovery to those whom they influence?

Interestingly enough, looking at the numbers, there were actually a number of them who expressed an initial interest when the topics revolved around substance and alcohol abuse, gambling, pornography, and the like. However, there was a *major* drop-off as soon as the discussion turned to food.

The reason, of course, was obvious.

When people begin to really look at the symptoms of the disease, it suddenly and very publicly suggests that addiction may be a possible tenant in a majority of the homes in the congregation– including some of those of the most prominent members or leaders.

The numbers simply mirror the national rates, but often have an unfortunate chilling effect on the conversation and the process.

Thankfully, as addiction is better understood, more and more compassionate leaders are getting involved. But it all began with the senior pastor at a small Lutheran congregation in Wisconsin, and one rabbi here in South Florida, who have been active promoters in making help, knowledge, and resources available to their members.

Not only am I sincerely grateful and filled with respect for them– but their people are blessed to have such faithful, caring and competent servants.

Others, however, are often tripped up by the flip side of the "willingness" coin, a side that can serve as a stumbling block to many professionals: pastors, priests, and rabbis– as well as physicians, counselors, and social workers alike.

It is the side of the coin stamped, "Able."

Willing and *able* are inseparable when it comes to generating results in any field, enterprise or endeavor, but they are especially crucial when it comes to identifying, diagnosing, and properly treating addiction.

Indeed, willingness to help, and ability to help, could mean the difference between life and death when working in any kind of addiction intervention or recovery– inside or outside the Church.

Please understand, this is no criticism of any particular denomination or religious body. To be sure, I'm not concerned with whether you pray this way or that, or what your burial traditions are.

I'm also not qualified to debate whether individual customs are ordinances, sacraments, or Divine commands. From where I sit, people can sing however they want, dress however they're comfortable, and dance, scream, chant or shout to their heart's desire.

Oh, and one other thing. I'm not worried about offending anyone's sensibilities by what I am going to say next, because I know without the slightest doubt– hands down– that I am living my mission and fulfilling the purpose that I was put on earth to do.

I help addicts *completely* recover from their addictions, and put their lives and relationships back together. And I believe that we should work as a team to help those in the Church.

Your church. Your synagogue. Your house of worship.

I say this out of love because, all too often, I've seen religious leaders, as well as elders and staff, fail individuals and families who are suffering from the devastating effects of addiction– and they're failing them at the very moment of their greatest vulnerability.

Addiction is a *medical* issue, not a spiritual or rebellion issue, and unfortunately, it is routinely being blown on *all* fronts. And while we will address the medical ramifications in more detail in an upcoming chapter, please know that members of the clergy can– and often do– get in over their heads when fighting this particular battle.

And it can happen quickly.

Now, I want you to understand that on a personal level, I don't dislike your priest. In fact, even without meeting them, I think it's safe to say that I'd probably love your pastor or rabbi.

But, from the standpoint of successfully leading a crisis intervention with a family that's teetering on the very brink of life and death with addiction, few clergy have undergone the *years* of specialized and intensive training required to avoid the critical mistakes that often come in such explosive environments.

And I realize this statement runs counter to the beliefs and expectations that many in the membership may have– they want to believe that the coursework and studies that their leaders took at Seminary or Rabbinical School prepared them for every crisis.

This not only places an unreasonable and unfair burden on the ministry team, but I have also witnessed the aftermath of a devastated family trying to pick up the pieces when the pressure cooker explodes, and I wish we had partnered with them sooner.

Here is what I believe:

I believe that God wants the addict in your life healed, and I believe that there are tools, resources, and actions that– when exercised in their proper form and in the proper sequence– allow that healing to occur.

Working together, complete recovery is available– for the individual, for the family, for the community– for the congregation.

POINT WELL TAKEN

We have spoken of the fact that any child alive today can get the point of *The Good Samaritan* story.

The listeners of that day did also.

But below the surface are several nuances that we must discuss, and a few questions that also come to mind.

First, remember that this entire lesson started when a student of the Law stood up and asked what he needed to do to be saved.

Saved, as in– you got it– *saved.*

Salvation: the "inherit eternal life" sorta saved.

Jesus replied by asking the lawyer how he understood it, and the man answered that he needed to love God completely, and his neighbor also. And Jesus– the guy who ought to know– responds affirmatively that the young man is absolutely correct.

The idea is that you cannot love God completely without *also* loving your neighbor– how interesting I find that!

But there's more.

Jesus then goes on to describe just who that neighbor is. Yes, it was so important to Jesus that his listeners knew that the Samaritan was *knowingly* helping a Jew– the enemy– that he put it in as the second word of His story:

"A *Jewish* man was traveling..."

To love God, then, means to also love "our enemies," and we know that we cannot be saved without loving God according to the confirmation that Jesus gave regarding this question.

And He didn't stop there. Jesus went on to give instruction on what it means to love our enemies: to be willing to stop and care for the basic needs of another, to the best of our ability.

In the simplest of terms, this is *The Samaritan Solution.*

And finally, after describing the conduct of the church workers who "passed by," He contrasted their behavior with that of the most despised man in the story, and asked, in effect, "So, who *really* loved their neighbor?"

In other words, who *really* loves God? Ouch...

How much louder and how much clearer can it be than that? These other men had grown up in the Yeshiva, been identified early on as Rabbinical candidates, memorized the Torah, dedicated their life to the service of the Lord, and are then ultimately told that some no-good outcast from Samaria now has God's favor because he cared for his enemy!

Now, here is what is important:

As believers, the expectation is no different for us today.

The command was clearly given in Scripture to carry the message of God's love for us– and His desire that we love others– to the ends of the earth, first to the Jews, then to all the Gentile world.

That means the lesson is for us, right now.

It doesn't matter how much we pray, what traditions we observe, or if we live, eat, and breathe in the church or synagogue— we have a responsibility to care for our fellow man, and that includes addiction.

WHAT WERE THEY THINKING?

So, I don't know about you, but before we leave this section, I sure would like to know what that whole "passing by" thing was all about anyway. Why on earth would these men have looked at a fellow Jewish brother and left him to die along the side of the road?

Over the years, several thoughts have emerged— all of which, not surprisingly, have applications for us as we learn to promote, encourage, and aid our neighbor's recovery from addiction.

Let's look at five possible explanations.

First was the thought that they were just in a hurry, and we understand that. Our own self-interest is certainly one of the key reasons that we avoid getting involved in a process of treatment that we don't really appreciate or understand.

Second was the idea that it may have been a Sabbath, and they needed to obey some kind of legalistic system that forbade them to get involved. This was clearly a notion that Jesus would not have identified with, as evidenced by his warning and rebuke.

Then there is a third theory, that they arrived too late, that the traveler had passed away. Under their belief system, to touch him would have made them unclean, and the ritual for regaining cleanliness was really quite time consuming, kind of a hassle, and especially so if all for naught. This hopelessness, that there is nothing that can be done, that it's just too late, also keeps many people today from getting involved.

And fourth, there is the fear factor. The religious workers could have been afraid to be ambushed themselves, or maybe they feared to be seen with a man who, for all they knew, could have been a criminal or someone who had brought this upon himself.

Whatever the reason, all too often today, we make similar judgments, relegating someone who is suffering great pain and illness to our own "untouchable" list.

Each of these four considerations is related to our *goodness*— our *willingness* to be involved.

The fifth consideration, on the other hand, is about *ability*. Maybe, just maybe, the pious travelers did not assist because they did not know how. Maybe they hadn't been trained in basic first aid, and didn't want to make matters worse.

Heck, it's even possible that they weren't really sure what they were even looking at. Maybe the severity of the situation just didn't register.

Of course, I'm giving them the benefit of the doubt, but this scenario is more common than you may realize. Many people today are living with addiction right under their noses, in their own homes, in their own lives, and they don't see what's going on until the disease begins to spiral out of control.

So, what *are* addiction's warning signs? Are they really that easy to spot? And where do we go from here?

Chapter 6

*   *   *

Caution: Danger Ahead

Let's play a game. And the winner gets... well, you'll find out at the end of the chapter!

In any event, say that you and a few of your family or friends were blindfolded and taken for a fast ride on the freeway. The driver takes a multitude of turns, then gets on a random Interstate and travels 70 MPH for seven hours or so in an unknown direction before all of your blindfolds are removed.

Okay, now go! How rapidly do you believe you could figure out where you were, and– maybe more importantly– where you were going?

Well, assuming you have an atlas and are paying attention, it won't likely take very long. After all, the signs on the road are everywhere!

For instance, if you see a sign that tells you that you're on I80W, and another informing you that Chicago is just ahead, it's pretty easy to figure out that if you just keep heading down the road– if you don't change a thing– Lincoln, Salt Lake City, and San Francisco are in your future.

Which is just fine, of course, if that's where you want to be.

But what happens when the signs start pointing in a direction that take you away from your desired destination? In that case, keeping your head down and your nose to the grindstone is a sure way to end up in a place that you never intended to go.

But it could be worse.

What if the signs start to indicate that there is serious trouble on the road ahead?

Often as we travel, signs are used to warn us, to urge caution, to help us avoid certain or potential danger. If we ignore those signs, we do so at our own peril, and to the detriment of those traveling with us.

Yes, in fact, there are certain roads which we should avoid altogether.

The road to addiction is one of them.

Now, here is what you need to know:

Contrary to public perception, the road to addiction isn't always a lonely and desolate trail. No, in fact, it may start out as the fun place to be. Both well-paved and busy, we may often get onto it from a very good part of town.

After all, it's where the party is, where the popular crowd hangs out. To be sure, the road to addiction doesn't necessarily begin as a torn-up, rocky road in the middle of nowhere.

But hear this– it *always* ends there.

And while there are many warning signs along the way, they are often camouflaged, only visible if you know what it is that you are looking for. Further, along the way, there is plenty of room to disregard the circumstances around us. We may even find ourselves outright denying that conditions around us are deteriorating.

After all, the road ahead can't be *that* bad– look how many others are going in the same direction!

Yes, the road to addiction can be wide and heavily traveled, if for no other reason than that there are so many things to which one may become addicted.

And as we have previously discussed, because all addiction ends with the destruction of the individual's health, relationships and finances, I want to help you recognize these warning signs, the symptoms of a disease that could otherwise steal your loved one's health, finances, relationships and life.

Now, let me be clear.

Once you have the skills to recognize the symptoms, you'll be able to see them anywhere. In fact, it may begin to seem as though they are everywhere! But it takes some time to develop this skill because addicts, and the countless numbers of enablers that often surround them, do everything possible to disguise the symptoms.

It is said that the hawk can spot a mouse from two miles away. With telescopic eyesight it searches the landscape and underbrush. Birds of prey are masters of their environment. Anything out of the ordinary will catch their attention, and from that moment on, their focus is on that object.

Yes, nature, with its predictable and steady course, objectively reveals those elements that are out of place. If something is wrong, it is evident.

Humanity, on the other hand, is often much more difficult to comprehend, simply because– as humans– we spend an inordinate amount of time sculpting the view that others see of us.

Public relations is big in America, and not just in the corporate world. We work diligently to shape the public image that goes before us and with us each day into work and play and relationships.

Need proof?

Well, don't raise your hand– just ask yourself quietly if you generally put a little extra effort into making the right first impression in a job interview, when meeting a brand new client, or going on that first date.

We all do.

We have been raised to put our best foot forward, cover our warts, and by all means allow family secrets to, well, remain secret.

And in family after family and generation after generation, we close the door to any and all discussion of such topics as substance abuse, alcoholism, and gambling. Conversations of anorexia, bulimia, and obesity are off limits, as are concerns over habits such as shopping or the use of pornography.

Addiction? Please– just keep it quiet.

SHARPENING YOUR VISION

Now, what if I told you that I could spot an addict from a mile away? Would you believe me? And if I said that it's just as simple without ever even meeting them personally, now how would you respond?

Crazy? Unbelievable? Impossible!

"Give me a break, Shelly! How can you claim to identify addiction without even meeting the addict? It's ridiculous!"

Okay, that's a reasonable question, and one that I will answer in just a minute. But before I do, I'd like to ask you to take a deep breath and settle down, because I also have a few questions for you.

This is so important to everything that happens with your friend or loved one from this point forward, so please consider the ramifications of this: what if I'm right?

And, more importantly, what if I could teach you to do the very same thing?

If it were possible to predict years in advance that, left unchecked, a friend or family member's current behavior would cause them to suffer a catastrophic illness and premature death, wouldn't you like to know?

Or, how about this...

What would you do if you knew with almost 100% certainty that one of your son's friendships would lead him to prison, or that all of the arguments in your home were really just one big lie, providing cover for hidden addictions?

Now, here's a flash– I have those insights every day.

You see, the road to addiction is littered with danger signs that are impossible to miss, if– and I'll say it again– if you know what to look for.

Any one of them, by itself, is cause for concern.

However, if several are present, you must take action.

No, let me rephrase: you must take *correct* action.

Remember the points made in the parable? The priest and the Temple worker also represented action– *wrong action* and *inaction.*

On the other hand, our Lord gave the example of an ordinary citizen, the lowly and despised Samaritan, taking correct and decisive measures to save the life of his fellow man.

This is our model. Loving God– and loving our neighbor.

As we saw earlier, at no time or place in this story did Jesus give any indication that our Samaritan friend was in any way uniquely qualified to do what he did.

We're told only that he had compassion. And yes, that he took action. That is the essence of *The Samaritan Solution.*

But first, he had to see the warning signs. He had to recognize the severity of his brother's condition, and understand that without his help right now, death was likely.

Yet, others had witnessed the same facts, even walked up for a closer look, only to turn back to their preoccupations. Back to their own thoughts and worries, their own cares and concerns, their careers and their travel and their time constraints.

The Samaritan, however, did not just see with his eyes. He also understood and comprehended the entire scene in a profoundly different way than those who had passed by earlier.

The Samaritan viewed life through the eyes of his heart.

And, as believers, it is through these eyes that we must view our relationships with our families and friends, our coworkers, and yes, even strangers.

After all, by Divine definition, they are our neighbors.

Yes, we need to see beneath the masks and the misfortunes, through the smokescreens and the status, past the symptoms and the excuses and the denial. We must recognize the warning signs that cry out from the silence in the lives of those privately struggling with addiction, those who are yearning for hope and help and are finding none.

As believers, and as our brother's keeper– as Good Samaritans– this is our work.

By now you know that addiction can only live in the dark. It can only exist when the warning signs go unnoticed, or when the danger signals are ignored.

Thankfully, as you will learn, the signs are pretty obvious. They could be financial, physical, mental, or emotional. Others are spiritual, social, relational or behavioral. We'll break these eight areas down, giving examples of each, and in the following chapter we'll learn to eliminate all those nasty mistakes that we spoke of in Part II, mistakes that– though born out of love and concern– have devastating and unintended consequences just the same.

So, as we look at these categories, let's remind ourselves that addiction always causes destruction. It always brings unexplained negative change. And, just like the hawk, it is often this unexplained change that you, as a family member or friend, will first notice– if you have your eye on the environment.

The point is this: if you notice *any* of the symptoms outlined in *any* of the following sections, that is your cue to investigate your concern, concern that is born out of Godly love for your fellow man.

Finally, please remember that the symptoms of addiction are very similar regardless of the type of addiction that is present, meaning that the person struggling with food or pornography or gambling is just as likely to exhibit any of these warning signs as an alcoholic or drug addict.

So, let's get started.

Let's look at the financial, physical, mental and emotional, spiritual, social, relational, and behavioral conditions which may foretell a disaster waiting around the next corner on the road to addiction.

FINANCIAL SIGNS OF ADDICTION

Some of the easiest signs to spot are in the area of finances, because quite frankly, you either have the cash or you don't!

Simple. So why do so many fail to notice?

Imagine– Joe was always so responsible with money, and he was so incredibly good in his career. But just last week, he got fired from his position, and for the first time in as long as anyone can remember, he has no prospects.

Now I can just hear someone saying, "Geez, Shelly, the economy's tough all over! *Lots* of people are getting laid off. Business is bad everywhere. Don't you know that?"

Well, maybe.

But a closer inspection might reveal another story.

A number of years ago, I was invited to help a Director of Human Resources identify a number of individuals who had addiction problems within his company. I told him, without a shred of doubt and absolutely no tongue in cheek whatsoever, that I could spot the addicts without ever meeting a single one.

Remember rolling your eyes when I brought this up a few pages back? Well, he laughed out loud... but not for long.

The process was really quite simple: just find out which employees had the thickest employment files. That's it. You'll find the files are packed for two types of individuals, both of whom have strong addictive tendencies.

First, we identified which ones were causing the most trouble– those who had the most reprimands, write-ups and warnings. You see, addiction often causes such behaviors to become pronounced. Please hear me: while these conditions are very noticeable, most people do not connect them with an underlying addiction, instead writing it off to issues of attitude or rebellion.

Second, we made note of those who, while seemingly cooperative and willing, just couldn't seem to deliver: those who were warm and friendly, but unreliable. Those who seem to live by Murphy's Law.

Murphy's Law?

Yes, you heard correctly.

With all due respect, I believe that Mr. Murphy was likely an addict!

You see, addicts live lives that are full of dysfunction, missteps, secrecy, and drama. Errors in judgment and behavior are common, and those errors explode in the areas of responsibility from time to time.

These need to be covered up, and often result in the creation of elaborate stories and actions to mask the truth. Find the drama, and more than likely, you've got your addicts.

The HR Director was stunned. We were 10 for 10.

There's no surprise here. Problems in the areas of work and finances are huge warning signals, though most blame them on something else.

You see, under that financial challenge, below the layoff or termination, is often a performance problem. Please, don't miss this– it's often your first clue. On the job, addiction *always* brings performance problems. Poor judgment, tardiness, disrespect. Missed days due to illness, lack of contribution or teamwork, the need for time off for unexplained "personal reasons."

Over time, others who don't have these issues will be promoted first, and have a greater chance of being kept on, especially when times are tough.

So yes, Joe lost his job. And his addiction remains hidden by the state of the economy, and the cadre of caring and loving family and friends, whom he counts on to carry his story for him.

Other financial signs that addiction may be present arise in a home when money suddenly seems to disappear. Maybe your spouse, child, or loved one can't explain where their funds have gone. Or worse, maybe it's your money that is suddenly missing from your purse or wallet, and you didn't spend it.

When push comes to shove, an addict will do whatever's necessary– beg, borrow, or steal– to get the resources that they need. You should know that many addicts turn to prostitution, almost for pennies, in an attempt to finance their addiction.

The addiction must be fed, and that always requires cash.

Additionally, subtle changes, such as bills that are not being paid on time, telephone calls from creditors, or an indifference to one's responsibilities to their personal or family finances should send up red flags immediately.

For a healthy individual, finances are fairly black and white, positive and negative, income and expenses. The sudden onset of issues, especially if combined with explanations of "bad luck," finger-pointing or half-truth is definitely reason for concern.

Start turning over some rocks, and you will often find that addiction is down there somewhere.

PHYSICAL SIGNS OF ADDICTION

When most people think of addiction and the warning signs that surround it, they typically identify the physical symptoms as those that are most recognizable.

This is not surprising, because the average American associates the word "addiction" with substance abuse– either drugs or alcohol. And while we might take issue with such a limited definition of addiction, we nonetheless recognize that it's out there, so let's go ahead and address it now.

We all know the effects that alcohol and drugs can have on the human body. The most obvious signs, of course, are sensory in nature– meaning those that we can smell, see or hear.

For example, if you meet your friend for lunch or your child comes home from school, and their breath or clothing reek of cigarettes, alcohol, or marijuana, there is little doubt about the activities in which they have recently been engaged.

This is not rocket science– it is cause for concern.

It should also be pointed out that as an isolated event, taken only by itself, such evidence means only that your loved one has been using these substances.

It doesn't necessarily mean that they are addicted to them.

However, these signs should not go unnoticed, and they certainly should not be disregarded.

Other physical signs may include red eyes, uncontrolled

shaking, or pale or flushing skin. These are all warnings of trouble ahead, as are the lack of balance, or the inability to speak or drive properly.

Each of these conditions indicate trauma to the nervous system caused by drugs and alcohol. But the real physical effects of addiction are far more devastating, far more long-term, and affect a far greater percentage of the population than just those who are abusing illicit drugs and alcohol.

Unfortunately, when it comes to addiction, most of the medical community– and, for that matter, most of our society– sees only the surface of such physical symptoms.

So they suspect that Billy is sleeping way too much, or too little. They see that Jenny has put on considerable weight or that Connie seems to have wasted away to nothing. They notice that Uncle Dan has no energy and has been sick an awful lot lately, but they don't seek to learn the reasons why.

However, the *most common* physical symptoms of addiction in America today are not the red eyes, the scent of pot or alcohol on the breath, or the other well-known signs of drug and alcohol abuse.

Not by a long shot.

As we now know, addiction to food affects more Americans than all other addictions combined, and is identified by the presence of heart disease, diabetes, cancer, stroke, high blood pressure, obesity, anorexia and bulimia.

Period.

Know anybody suffering with any of these?

"Now wait, Shelly– are you saying my *mom* is a food addict?"

No. You said that.

I'm just spreading the good news that medical science has

pinpointed three food categories that cause the pancreas to overproduce insulin in almost 70% of the population, resulting in a host of illnesses and premature death.

To some, I suppose that's bad news. I took it as good news, and I didn't fight the diagnosis. I accepted it, and did something about it– and as a result, I'm in great health and 183 pounds lighter than I once was.

But the physical symptoms don't stop with with alcohol, drug, and food addiction.

Addiction of any kind puts measurable stress on the body's immune and regulatory systems, causing significantly shortened lifespans and unnecessary illness.

Additionally, there are several other physical warning signs that should get your attention. Often, addictive behavior causes sexual side effects that manifest in the loss of interest and intimacy within relationships.

For example, impotency in men is a side effect of many of the common illnesses that we have previously discussed, as well as the result of the mental and emotional destruction that comes from various addictions.

And the advice from the medical and pharmaceutical experts?

Well, of course, they will spend a fortune on advertising to suggest that you run right to your doctor's office and ask for a sample of a little blue pill, or whatever color the marketing people believe is currently the most attractive.

And it's unfortunate, because once again addiction got away.

MENTAL & EMOTIONAL SIGNS OF ADDICTION

As troublesome as the physical signs of addiction are, the mental and emotional signs can be even more disheartening. You see, as a rule, there is widespread trust in our society that *physical* illnesses and challenges can be corrected.

We see it happen all the time.

So we learn that cousin Elizabeth *had* pneumonia last year, Joan's friend David *had* a strange case of non-specific posterior rash, or William wasn't at work last week, because he *had* his knee replaced.

Had, had, had. And then they got better.

However, we have far less faith that one's mental and emotional problems can be cured. They are much less predictable, and often volatile. The diagnosis and the cure, if there is to be one, often seems to take a very experimental tone.

So, we find that someone is depressed, having trouble sleeping, experiencing panic attacks– all common side effects and danger signs of addiction. Someone should notice.

Instead, what happens? "Try this pill," we're told.

And if that doesn't work?

"Well, then we'll try that one."

I've got a better idea: why don't we *try* to get at the root of the problem! Because if we find that the cause of the mental and emotional roller coaster is addiction, then there is a very good chance for complete and total recovery.

Yes, you heard correctly: complete and total recovery.

Now, if you have a family member, friend, or loved one exhibiting these symptoms, that last statement just got your attention.

So what *do* those danger signals look like anyway? What mental or emotional traits may indicate a completely recoverable addictive condition?

As mentioned earlier, addiction causes changes in the brain, affecting hormonal and chemical balances that regulate not only our moods, but also our very ability to function as loving or caring individuals in our relationships and as productive members of society.

When addiction is present, you may notice any or all of the following warning flags. In fact, let me state it in reverse: if you do notice *any* of these symptoms, suspect addiction of one sort or another somewhere.

It is important to understand that seldom do these warning signs show up without bringing others along with them. As an addict begins to see the manifestations of a financial or physical slide, or the destruction in their spiritual, social or relational life that we will speak of shortly, this stress can cause confusion, anxiety, depression or mania.

It is not uncommon for your friend or loved one to experience profound anger, sadness, or thoughts of suicide.

Blackouts, paranoia, or forgetfulness can also accompany the extreme highs and lows associated with addiction. This creates an intensely worrisome situation for us as friends or family members, and also presents a clear and present danger to the public if our loved one operates machinery, spends any time behind the wheel, or cares for others.

SPIRITUAL SIGNS OF ADDICTION

At the center of ourselves, is– well– ourselves.

Our spiritual nature is our connection to God, and it is also the keeper and guardian of our self-image.

It is who we are, who we really are, when no one else is around. We have spoken thus far of the destruction of an addict's physical and emotional life, but these cannot begin to compare to the destruction of his or her spiritual life. Left alone, here the destruction of the individual as a person is made complete.

I haven't pleaded with you up to this point, but I will do so right now.

If you find these characteristics present in someone that you care about– no matter what they say, regardless of any reason they give you, or how scared or inadequate you feel in dealing with this– please understand that, almost certainly, you are engaged with addiction in one form or another.

You must reach out for help and you must do so now.

The most recognizable spiritual signs that you are dealing with issues of addiction are an overarching sense of hopelessness, the feeling that there's no use in trying, or a sense of lack of control over one's life. Thoughts of suicide are common as the individual gives up on the future.

The neglect of core values, the loss of self-worth and extreme feelings of guilt, shame, fear or abandonment live here. Please understand– if this sounds at all familiar, put this book down now and contact me personally with the information found at the back of this book.

This is as thin as the ice gets– without professional help, your loved one may not survive this.

SOCIAL SIGNS OF ADDICTION

Well, your mom always told you, watch who you're hanging around with. And it turns out that Mom was pretty wise. That's not just good advice for children, either– it is also instructive for adults, and can be helpful in identifying either healthy or addiction-friendly relationships.

You see, we tend to hang around people just like us.

So, chances are that even if you and I have never been introduced, if I spend a day with each of your three closest friends, in effect I've likely met you, too. Similar habits, similar thoughts, similar values.

So how does this apply to addiction?

Well, if you know that your son is hanging out with the crowd who smokes dope regularly, it is probable, regardless of what he tells you, that they accept him and he accepts them because they're involved in many of the same activities... in this case, the dope.

If you know that your sister and her husband spend most of their free time with friends who gamble regularly, despite the financial trouble they're in– or if you know that your father's best friends are not just his coworkers, but they are also alcoholics– well, where there's smoke, there's usually fire.

Remember Mildred from a few chapters back? All of her associations shared her addiction to sugar, all were overweight, and all would eventually contract the diabetes that would shorten their lives significantly.

These are clearly danger signs on the road to addiction.

Other social signs that merit concern might include friendships that appear to be based on risk-taking, loud, obnoxious, or out-of-control mannerisms and disrespect for societal authority.

It is very common for those dealing with addiction to suddenly take part in activities that are criminal in nature, and be associated with those who routinely have run-ins with the law.

If you are troubled by the associations and social interactions of your loved ones, or if you suspect or know that there are addicts amongst their friends, it is reasonable to suspect the same for your friend or family member.

RELATIONAL SIGNS OF ADDICTION

"It never used to be this way. Bobby was so happy, such a good kid. I don't know where we went wrong, but he doesn't seem to even want to see us anymore."

Or how about these?

"My husband never used to act this way. He used to be so nice. I don't know what's happened, but it's like we're living in two different worlds."

"Roberta's been so sick the last few years. And she's gained so much weight and seems so unhappy. She never goes anywhere anymore."

If you've ever said those words, or heard those words said by someone close to you, then you have witnessed the relational signs of addiction. As the disease progresses, it saps the vitality from its victims, leaving them a shell of their former self.

Unfortunately, the relational changes are often so slow or hidden that the slide is not easily recognized while it is happening. Only when we look back over time and compare the way it was to the way it is now do we notice the difference.

You've likely heard the story of the frog that is placed in cold water on the stove. As the temperature slowly rises, the frog moves not an inch– until, alas, the frog is boiling. My coauthor, Steve, has a friend who says it's an interesting and cute little metaphor– until you realize that you, or someone you care about deeply, is the frog.

Relational signs of addiction often begin with a gradual withdrawal from friends and family. You may notice that where once your loved one was active, engaged, even highly opinionated, they are suddenly quiet and reserved.

You may notice that subjects or hobbies that were once so important to them now seem to carry very little weight, commanding minimal interest or attention.

They are less willing to share their life, avoiding direct answers to even basic questions, especially if they feel you would not approve of their activities or lifestyle.

This is an area where a discerning pastor, rabbi or ministry worker may first recognize a potential addictive situation with one of their members. As addiction changes behavioral patterns, the victim searches for more and more ways to hide what is going on. They may suddenly stop attending services, stop returning phone calls, or be unresponsive to pastoral care.

Without an understanding of addiction, it is easy to see this withdrawal as intentional rebellion or apathy toward spiritual matters. In these cases, many congregations have a process that is designed to either quickly force the individual back into the fold or lay the foundation for the member's removal from the roster– at the very moment when an addict's need for support may be the greatest.

While it is natural to feel hurt, frustrated, or even angry because of the individual's actions, it is important to realize that they may not be willingly turning their back on you. Addiction, as a disease, seeks to eliminate the competition.

One of which is you.

This phase can be quite draining on all of the relationships involved, especially when combined with the behaviors we will discuss next. Keep in mind that your loved one is still in there, but they need help to eliminate the poison which has encircled their life.

BEHAVIORAL SIGNS OF ADDICTION

So, you have enough information to suspect that there's a real problem here, and you muster up all the courage you can to speak with your friend, your sister, your mother, or your son. You want to let them know that you love them, and care for them, and will do whatever it takes to help them.

And then they'll collapse in your arms, and apologize through their tears, and you can just sense that healing and recovery and happiness are right around the corner... right?

Well, no. Not if you've locked horns with addiction.

Unfortunately, rather than the love-fest described above, you are much more likely to get one of the three behavioral signs of addiction:

Blame, deceit, or *denial.* And, just for good measure, they usually come wrapped in *anger.* Now, we covered the family's use of these behaviors earlier in the book, but they hold a very special place in the life of the addict.

We'll discuss that here.

You'll find that anger is the opposite and aggressive side of the withdrawal coin. If the addict can't easily *pull away* from you, then *pushing you away* may be the answer. Anger starts arguments for no reason at all, and those fights are then used to justify the addiction.

Anger is at the heart of blame.

Blame seeks to make you the enemy, to unload the addict's responsibility onto you. In case you've never been there, let me tell you how it sounds, so that you can identify this sure sign of addiction:

"This is all your fault! Ohhh, you make me so mad, it's no wonder I drink (or eat or smoke or gamble). Nothing I ever do is good enough for you! Just get off my back for once!"

Now see, wasn't that easy? And all because you dared to express your love.

In comparison to blame, which seeks to redirect responsibility, deceit takes a different tack. It seeks to deflect attention away by minimizing the activity in the first place.

Deceit says, "There was no alcohol at the party," or "I only did it one time, and that was ages ago."

Here's a medley of my personal favorites: "I promise this was the last time. I'm so sorry... I will quit immediately. I swear on my life, on my mother's life, that I will never do it again."

Ever been there?

Then two months or two weeks or two days later, they're right back at it. Or, in an effort to maintain their promise, many addicts will merely switch the substance or activity of choice.

So, Robert quit drinking, but now he smokes like a chimney. Thank goodness Cheryl finally quit smoking, but she eats until she secretly throws up. And Gordy sure does drink a lot more since he quit going to the casino.

Deceit is a vicious circle.

It looks you straight in the eye, and tells you that what you see as a problem is *not really* what you see.

And you must be ready for this. If pushed, deceit often turns into anger and blame. And how you handle that may have a great influence on the eventual recovery or demise of the person you love.

Here's a fun old saying– "It's not just a river in Egypt!"

Yes, our old friend, Mark Twain, seemed to know a little bit of something about almost everything, and his comment above was proof. Of course, he was speaking about the addict's oldest and dearest friend, denial.

Denial is interesting because it actually admits the activity– it just won't admit that it's an issue. Denial boldly proclaims, "This is not a problem. I can quit whenever I want! Besides, I just like having a little in moderation. The truth is that I really don't even want to stop."

Now, let me be very clear about this: if your genuine concern and caring is met with blame, deceit, denial, and anger– if your home or your relationships are weighed down with arguments and fighting– you are likely dealing with addiction.

No, I'll go further than that, and say that you *are* dealing with addiction– and you can come and rub my nose in it in the unlikely and miniscule chance I am wrong.

The only question is addicted to what?

And if, as you've listened, other warning signs have been piling up with your loved one's finances, with their health, with their mental and emotional condition, with their spiritual and social lives, if their relationships are falling apart, let me say it again: you *are* dealing with addiction, and you *will* need a plan.

You should know there are no cookie cutter solutions, no textbook or do-it-yourself quick-fix programs. There is no one-size-fits-all CD solution that you can listen to and go save a life.

A successful recovery plan for your situation will be as customized as the situation itself. And if it is going to work, it must be based on your specific issues, your family dynamics, and the individual strengths and weaknesses of each person involved.

So, what about that game we started at the beginning of this chapter– you know, the one where you're blindfolded and heading down the trail of life? Suddenly, you can see, and better yet, you can now read the signs.

You know where you are, and more importantly, you know where you're going.

Best of all, you've recognized the danger, and you've decided to get your family, your friend, your relationship, onto a different path.

Congratulations– you're about to trade the road to addiction for the road to recovery. Your life, and that of your loved one, will never be the same.

What a great game! And the winner gets... the life of their loved one back again.

And you begin playing on the next page.

Chapter 7

* * *

Compassion And Action

Okay, here is what I believe...

No, let's try that again: here is what I know.

If it weren't for the fact that I'm an abstinent gambler for over forty years, I would bet you $50 right now that you didn't read all the way through six previous chapters just so you could feel sorry for yourself or your loved one.

I bet I won that bet!

And here's what else I know:

You didn't spend the money to buy this book just to get some sugar-coated, rose-colored gobbledygook about how if we just all learn to listen a little better and tolerate a little more, everything is going to work out all right and we can be singing Kumbaya around the campfire this time next year.

No, in fact, that would probably be a good book with which to start the fire! But, alas, I digress.

Now, here is what *you* know:

Addiction is nasty and raw, and it is right now redefining every one of your relationships in which it is involved. It's the reason for the increased doctor visits, the stress and anxiety of the holidays, and the uncertainty of the future with a friend or family member that you love dearly.

And here is what else you know:

You've tried just about everything you can think of. You're pulling your hair out and you're at your wits' end.

The title of this chapter, "Compassion And Action," comes directly from our parable– in fact, it is at the very heart of the story of *The Good Samaritan.*

"...and when he saw the man, he felt compassion for him. Going over to him, the Samaritan soothed his wounds with olive oil and wine and bandaged them.

Then he put the man on his own donkey and took him to an inn, where he took care of him. The next day he handed the innkeeper two silver coins, telling him, 'Take care of this man. If his bill runs higher than this, I'll pay you the next time I'm here.'"

Now, forget everyone and everything else for a moment. Yes, forget the circumstances. Forget what was going on with the other players in our story. I want you to put out of your mind our Jewish traveler. I want you to cast aside any relevance of the bandits, and for Pete's sake, let's stop blaming the priest and Temple worker!

There is only one focus of the remainder of this book, and that is the compassion and the action of the Samaritan... the solution.

Right now, let's talk for just a minute about exactly what the Scriptures *did not* say.

The story *does not* say, for example, that, "When he saw the man, he felt *sympathy* for him."

No, no, no– it says that our hero felt *compassion.*

What's the difference, you ask?

Well, clearly– the life of your loved one.

You see, sympathy is defined as, *"A feeling or an expression of pity or sorrow for the distress of another."*

Pity or sorrow.

So break it down. Pity is described as, "A *matter of regret*," and sorrow as, *"Mental suffering or pain caused by injury, loss, or despair."*

Why the clarification?

Because while those may be the feelings, thoughts, and emotions that often dominate the lives of those who are living with addiction– indeed, while they may very well be the uninvited guest in your home as you read this now– they *are not* the feelings, thoughts, and emotions that drove the Samaritan to take action that day on the Jericho road!

And they *are not* the model the Lord laid out for you and me.

Now get this, Believer... for it is a matter of life and death.

Scripture is very precise.

It says, "...and when he saw the man, he felt *compassion*."

Compassion.

What a beautiful word.

Compassion is to sympathy as the Cavalry is to a stranded, solitary, and wounded soldier.

Compassion is defined as, *"A deep awareness of the suffering of another coupled with the wish to relieve it."*

In other words, compassion is going to do something!

And that is the Scriptural model.

Do you see the difference?

While sympathy cries, "This is horrible! I'm so sorry. I feel so bad for you, but I just don't know what to do," compassion boldly proclaims, "Yes, this is terrible, and it is not going to continue as long as I have anything to say about it!"

It is the heart of *The Samaritan Solution!*

And it is the decision you have before you today.

You see, the choice to act is not up to the addict.

It is up to you.

FAMILY AFFAIR

I think when you have a calling, you just naturally attract people that need or want what you have. At times, as I think of the thousands of people I've met, something always amazes me: there is one behavior that they all seem to share.

It doesn't matter whether they're young or old, or whether they're black, white, red, yellow or green. For that matter, married, single, widowed, or divorced, all political and religious persuasions or none at all, the conversation always seems to take the same track.

Yes, as different as people can be, it's incredible how often I hear the same few words within minutes of our introduction.

"Wow, really? You're an addiction counselor? Oh, I know someone who could really use your help! I'll pass along your name and number."

Or, how about this one: "I'll speak with them and see if they're interested, and then I'll get back to you."

Amazing.

The only change over the years is that, today, with new technologies and everyone connected in so many different ways, I hear it in many more venues now: comments on my website, in my e-mail, on Facebook and social media. And in the future, who knows? Wherever people connect, we'll be there.

But here's how it sounds:

"This is so great, Shelly! I just *know* you can help them! I mean, I sure *hope* you can help them. Oh man, they really *need* someone to help them– I'll have 'em call you."

Now, please... those are nice sentiments.

And yes, I understand that you truly desire to help. But you must hear what I am about to say next, because addiction is not only a matter of life and death, it is also a matter of timing.

And if *you* do not help them, the situation *will* get worse, and there is a strong likelihood that you will lose them.

Let me rephrase and repeat just to make this as simple as possible:

If you do not help them, you will probably lose them.

And that is so unnecessary.

There are three things I want to share with you this very minute– some bad news, some good news, and a decision that you need to make.

First, the bad news:

If addiction really is at the root of the problem, having read this far, you must know by now that the addict is not looking for help. Not from you, and certainly not from me.

Regardless of what they're into, they have already tried many times to control it or stop it, and they can no longer see living the next 24 hours, no less the rest of their lives, without it.

You can give them one hundred phone numbers– they aren't going to call.

Next, the good news:

I know that you may think your situation is different, and I know you may believe you've tried it all, but here is the message– the gift– that I bring to you today.

I have *never* met an addict who could not be helped... *if*– and this is another big if– *if* we got to them before it was too late.

Let me say it again: I have never met an addict who could not be helped– never, not one– if we got to them in time.

And this is the point.

This is why *you* need to make the decision.

After all, you are the one reading the book.

If you have even skimmed these pages, glanced at the powerful testimonies on my website, or downloaded any of the free resources there, you already know more about the process and potential for recovery than any of your friends and family combined.

Someone needs to be the hero. Someone needs to have compassion. Yes, someone needs to take action– and that someone, that Samaritan, is you. And, all too often and unfortunately, many families wait until it is too late to reach out and get help.

Because addiction is always progressive, by now you know that, without treatment, it always gets worse. You know it won't stop with your relationships; you know it won't stop with the finances; you know it will demand your loved one's life; and it will likely sap the energy from yours in the process.

And yet, so many families resist.

It may be rooted in their own guilt, embarrassment, or shame– or in their desire to control it themselves or keep a lid on it. It could be that their own denial keeps them from admitting the truth and severity of their loved one's illness, condition, and prognosis for the future.

Regardless, I've seen families spend *years* doing nothing.

Decades, in fact!

Or, as stated earlier, they give out my phone number and suggest the addict call, which, while it feels good for the moment, is really doing just next to nothing.

You see, the addict does not act responsibly. We already know that.

The addict is in denial. We know that, too.

And therefore, the addict is not going to pick up the telephone and make the call. If you don't already know that, you very soon will.

Now, please accept this with the love in which it is offered:

There is help for your loved one, and yes, they really can have their hope, their future, and their life back. You can have them back. But it won't happen by sending short and sweet text messages. Your friend or neighbor or relative isn't going to reach out to connect with me or any other professional by e-mail or Facebook or Twitter.

And, the real truth is, it's *not* going to happen without you.

Now, I know this can be a hard message for families to take, but we've already discussed that. And you are not just *anyone* in the family. You are a *leader* in the family, and a soon-to-be hero.

We've already settled this issue: we're here to save the life of someone you love. Kumbaya can wait.

But as we lay out a three point plan for recovery, you need to know that you are going to be challenged– certainly by the addict in your life, but also by other friends and family who are hurt, angry, or confused.

As this heats up– as it always does– you will likely find that not everyone on the team is cut out for the task at hand. And it doesn't matter what addiction your loved one is struggling to overcome. As life gets difficult, someone in the family or inner circle almost certainly begins looking for "an easier way to do this."

And, unfortunately, there are plenty of things one can "try."

To be sure, there is no shortage of people out there willing to take your money for "easy" solutions to one of the world's most difficult and destructive problems.

You can find books and seminars and DVD home-study programs, supplements and herbs and a million and one websites.

Anything to separate you from your wallet is fair game to marketers, who prey off the pain and willingness of families and friends to try just about anything.

Don't fall for them.

CAVEAT EMPTOR

As laid out in an 1817 U.S. Supreme Court decision, *caveat emptor,* or "let the buyer beware," became the principle in commerce that places sole responsibility on the buyer to assess the truth, quality or usefulness of a product or service before purchasing.

Of course, this doctrine assumes that the buyer is capable of making such a sound judgment in the first place, which in the case of someone suffering from addiction is a highly questionable assumption.

Sadly, families and individuals who are neck-deep in substance abuse– or the addictive activity of their choice– are often at great risk of making serious errors as they grasp for anything that remotely resembles straws of hope.

I relate the following story to you because these are the types of situations that you are going to run into as family and friends begin to search for outside options and opinions that can spare them some of the emotional investment and misery that is typical during recovery.

Unfortunately, many caring and concerned people– including those in your circle– may fall for these types of scams. Scams which hurt the effort in a number of ways:

First, they drain the family's finances, leaving fewer resources for legitimate alternatives that would aid recovery.

Second, as these programs inevitably fail, they demoralize and frustrate both the addict and the family, each of whom become less likely to make future attempts using even the most proven and effective means.

And third, they eat up precious time, damaging the addict's

health at the very moment when there may be little or no time to spare.

Please hear this:

You must be aware that many good people, victims of addiction, die because they and their family and friends are playing games with recovery.

I can tell you in no uncertain terms that *if* you play, you *will* lose.

Period.

Would you like an example to drive home the point?

Here is the kind of nonsense that is marketed out there– a type of bad joke that could literally claim your loved one's life...

A short time ago, I heard a radio advertisement that was being billed as a one-size-fits-all, at-home recovery program, to be sent on twenty-four Compact Disks– and specifically designed for those with an alcohol addiction.

"It's confidential, completely private, and it works fast!"

Yes, fast– as in 24 days.

That was my first red flag.

The best rehabs in the country, those who have advanced teams of professionals working personally with your loved one, wouldn't bet they could pull that off.

Just imagine– an alcoholic, killing themselves for years, completely dependent, kicking the addiction in little more than a few weeks.

But you see, I understand.

I understand you desire the changes. I understand you want to avoid the confrontation. I understand you long for your mom or dad, son or daughter, friend or fiancé to be well again.

But it doesn't work that way.

And yes, I know that if you look long enough and hard

enough you can find a few rehab programs that will accept your loved one– and your money– for very brief periods. However, I doubt they'd stake their state license on the long-term result. In fact, maybe that would be a good question to ask them.

And sad as it may be, the truth is that the main reason the 14- and 28-day rehab programs even exist is because that's what the insurance company said they would pay for. Unfortunately, they'll likely be paying again later, after it doesn't work this time.

Count on it.

So, the point is, if a fully staffed and trained rehab couldn't set things straight that quickly, how could a CD program do it?

I figured I should probably find out.

"Call right now for your free informational CD!" the ad proclaimed.

So, I did.

This is where my second red flag went up.

When I asked for my CD, the "consultant"– or, in this case, salesperson– on the other end of the phone launched into an amateurish presentation with a dozen scripted "closing questions," finally culminating with this gem of an exchange:

"So, Shelly, are you the person who is drinking too much, or are you concerned for someone else?"

"Someone else. And by the way," I asked, "where's the part where I get my free informational CD?"

"Okay," she said, avoiding my question, "so if I can just get *their* address, and *your* credit card number, we'll go ahead and bill you the $495, and we'll also send the program out to the alcoholic's house today so that they can 'inspect' it for 30 days. And there's absolutely no risk to you, because *if* they return it within that time, we'll refund your credit card– so, which card will you be using?"

Right.

You know, if there weren't so many families struggling with addiction that could potentially get sucked into this, it might actually be funny.

Just think about it:

Through all the hatred, and all the anger, the depression, the vitriol, the blame and deceit and denial, my addicted family member goes to the door one Tuesday afternoon and receives a package "in a plain brown wrapper"– a program he didn't order, didn't ask for, doesn't want and doesn't think he needs.

Then he'll listen– with discipline– to exactly one CD per day for the next twenty-four days, follow all the instructions to the letter, and see the error of his ways.

Yes, and he'll become aware of all that he's been missing out on, all the pain he's caused and change his life for the better.

Uhh... right.

Or else, he'll take advantage of the "no-risk" guarantee. Realizing that the program is "just not for him," he'll take care– through the cloud of his addiction– to carefully re-wrap the contents and get it to the Post Office on time so that his wretched loved one– in this case, me– who he is currently fuming at, won't be charged almost five hundred dollars.

Uh... huh.

Caveat emptor.

So what is a family to do, and what is this three-pronged approach that I mentioned earlier?

Good questions, seeing it will almost certainly mean the difference between fighting this battle forever, or returning your home to an environment of love and sanity.

And I am happy to answer them. In fact, it is the reason for the book. But first, I have a question for you:

Are you looking for information– or transformation?

I ask the question because in the last forty years or so I have witnessed countless families take the same information you are receiving today and...

Put it into immediate action? Well, actually... no.

Apply it to their own lives to rescue their loved one? Nope.

Distribute it to others who could become an important part of the recovery team? Nada.

Spread the good news to others in need? You get the picture.

No, instead good people with good hearts who have broken families and every reason under the sun to act, take this information, and bury it.

The same thing they will do with their loved one within the next thirty-six months or so.

And that leads me to ask again:

Information– or transformation?

Because, very often, the only difference between the two is a hero's willingness to act. You see, ever-increasing amounts of information without a plan for application will simply result in a muddying of the waters. Additional confusion, at the very moment when clarity is needed.

You, Believer, must provide the clarity.

You must act.

Your family member or friend– indeed, all of your family members– will thank you later.

Remember that it was the Samaritan's *actions* that transformed the victim's life, and, along with it, a little piece of history. All the pity, sorrow, and sympathy in the world would have changed nothing. The victim would have died, and there would have been no story to tell.

No example to set. No hope for the hurting, then or now.

OPTIONS, OPTIONS

I just Googled the phrase, *Addiction Help*, and it looks like I may be up all night. You see, my initial search turned up 167,000,000 results. Now, I can't say for sure, but I suspect there will likely be even more in the future.

So I refined my search.

Addiction Help Dallas, was better– but not really by much. There were 10,900,000 results returned.

Atlanta, 11,800,000.

Boston, 19,100,000.

New York City, 127,000,000.

Yes, if I needed help right now it would be a long night, indeed! How can one process all of that?

And the truth is, if there were just twenty options to consider, that is still more than most families can handle at a time when stress is at an all-time high, relationships are stretched to their breaking point, and the answers to recovery are clouded by confusion and marred by arguments among family members.

When Timmy is no longer talking to Mom and Dad, when Rachel hasn't been seen in weeks, or when the lab work just came back with bad news for Aunt Betty, it's difficult to have a nice family roundtable discussion on the topic of addiction– about all of its causes and solutions.

Here's why...

Timmy doesn't want to hear it.

Rachael isn't going to be there.

And Betty won't admit she has a problem.

Regardless, the solution to your family's crisis is no secret...

It is within reach, and it must come in three distinct parts:

1) Proper medical intervention,
2) Twelve Step fellowship, and
3) Individual, group, and family counseling.

Now, please hear what I said, and also what I *did not* say.

I said that there was one solution, and it *must come* in three distinct parts. I *did not* say that you had your choice of three separate and distinct solutions.

What's the difference, you ask?

Well, by following what I *did* say– versus what I *did not* say– you have a 3100% greater chance of saving the life of the person that you love. And where I come from, that's worth listening to.

"Okay, Shelly– so what I hear you saying is that *some* treatment plans aren't very successful, is that correct?"

No, I'm saying that *most* of what you'll find out there is *completely useless,* and even the most legitimate rehabs, Twelve Steps, and counselors achieve only about a 3% success rate when considered independently. *Three percent.*

Now, imagine for just a moment any other product or service that had such incredibly lousy numbers!

Would you buy a car that only started 3% of the time, or pay for braces from an orthodontist who boasted of that success rate? How confident would you feel about a surgical procedure if the doctor suddenly informed you that only three in one hundred patients actually survive the surgery?

"What?!" you'd be thinking. "This is totally experimental!"

And you'd be right.

You see, taken by themselves, none of these solutions is really a long-term fix.

Yes, the rehab will get Mom to quit binging, and you bet, Tyler will stop using, while he's locked up in an inpatient facility. However, once completed, our family member or friend is then released back into the very environment that promotes the use of whatever it was that landed them in rehab in the first place.

Next, Twelve Step Programs are great, but they are typically filled with kind, wonderful folks who are struggling to maintain their own sobriety in one addiction, while they're busy picking up another. It's our old example of breaking the alcohol or gambling addiction, only to die of diabetes or heart disease that was brought on by a hidden and untreated food addiction.

And finally, counseling in and of itself generates the same 3% as all the others, especially if it is only the addict who is being seen. Yet, this is where many families would like their loved one's recovery to begin and end. They reach a point where they are just so frustrated that they simply want to drop the addict on someone else's doorstep and leave them there.

I understand why you want to do that, but I care enough to tell you the truth. It's not that simple, so take a deep breath and we'll walk through each part together.

A DOCTOR IN THE HOUSE

Several years ago, I spoke at a conference on addiction that was attended by many of the most well-regarded and highly-esteemed professionals in the country.

To my amazement– and, no doubt, to many others whose primary focus is on the treatment of addiction– a number of the physicians and care workers from the medical community expressed the belief that too much time and effort was being devoted that particular weekend to the subject of addiction.

Excuse me? It was a conference on *addiction!*

Now, don't get me wrong.

These were good people– doctors, nurses, social workers, along with many other therapy professionals. But they had no idea of addiction's saturation into our society. In their own words, addiction cases are certainly an "occasional evil, but definitely not one that's prevalent in our society, in our city or in our practice."

Hmm...

The most stunning remarks came from the director of a prestigious East Coast medical school, who spoke of treating only three addicts in his entire and illustrious thirty year practice.

Three addicts... in thirty years!

"Of those," he stated quite matter-of-factly, "two were easily treated with success– we found that they just needed to cut back a bit. And unfortunately, we lost the other patient."

Oh well. You win some, and lose some.

Que sera sera...

I'm sorry, that's not acceptable!

From my experience, it is likely that there were *no* addicts successfully treated in that man's practice.

By every description, in the two "successful" cases that he reported, each had recently experienced high-stress events, to which they responded by increased drinking.

While this was certainly not the proper response on their part, there was nothing to indicate that they were indeed addicts, and the doctor's admonition to "cut back a bit" was sufficient.

However, the third individual, the true addict, was not helped. A physician's recommendation to an addict to cut back is no more useful than telling you or me to cut back on oxygen.

An addict needs the drink, the drug, the food, the gambling– like we need to inhale and exhale.

Worse, it is possible that hundreds or thousands of people have been through that medical practice over the years, and addiction was never even considered in an analysis seeking the root cause of their physical and emotional challenges.

For example, the patient presents with a history of alcohol or substance abuse, a track record of destructive behavior and damaged relationships, and there is no mechanism for the doctor to get to the cause.

Addiction remains hidden.

So the patient is prescribed something for anxiety– maybe that will reduce their stress level and they can then "cut back a bit."

It doesn't work.

Or the patient comes in eighty pounds overweight, or maybe it's one hundred eighty, and there is no process available to get to the root of their food addiction. So, they are lectured or threatened, put on a pill, or offered the name of a specialist who would be happy to go in and remove a good part of their stomach to control their appetite!

Just one question:

How does the pill, the surgery, or the verbal dressing-down heal the guilt, shame, embarrassment, or fear that is driving the addiction?

Answer: they don't.

And as the causes are missed, the behaviors continue– and eventually their relationships, along with their physical, emotional, and spiritual health are destroyed.

Now, please understand, this is not meant to say that good medical intervention doesn't have an integral part to play in recovery from addiction.

On the contrary, it is a critical component, along with the Twelve Step fellowship programs and the counseling that we will discuss in more detail shortly.

In fact, I cannot overstate the benefit that the patient receives when doctors, therapists, families, and community form a team that plans, executes, and supports the recovery of an individual.

On the other hand, remove any one of the components, and, as we've seen, the success rates plummet to about 3%.

Unfortunately, many doctors will confide privately that substance abuse or addiction medicine was not a significant focus of their training, nor is it a strength in their practice.

They just don't know what to do.

For the purposes of our future discussions, then, let's define proper and effective medical intervention as that which stops the addict from using, while at the same time setting the stage for aftercare that includes the restructuring of life and thought patterns for both the individual and their family through ongoing Twelve Step support and counseling.

Please know that this three-pronged approach– proper medical intervention, Twelve Step fellowship, and counseling– has been proven in thousands of cases to produce successful recovery rates in excess of ninety-six percent, wherever and whenever it is used correctly.

And when the stakes are this high, when your family's future is on the line, nothing less is acceptable.

So, where do you find medical professionals who really understand addiction? Where can you go to find physicians who can speak with you, answer your concerns, and provide a map that details both the scope and limitations of their services?

Not surprisingly, you'll likely find them working in association with the top rehab facilities in the country. After all, that is all they do at a rehab. They've got to be good at it– right?

Well, you might be surprised.

As you recall, any of the components alone yield about a 3% recovery rate, and at 3%, the best rehabs don't fair much better than the worst.

After all, there is not a big difference between 3% and 0%.

And furthermore, how would you know the "best" anyway?

Good question.

Now, I just Googled the phrase, *Best Rehab*, and I want you to know that it's going to be an even longer night!

The question of "best" is a difficult one to answer, because as technology advances are made, as people and staff come and go, the treatment quality is undoubtedly affected, positively or negatively.

Often, your best resource may be a good counselor who can assist you in coordinating a treatment plan and facilities that meet the needs of both you and your loved one, while also considering the time, emotional, and the financial impacts as well.

Now, speaking of finances, I find it very interesting that in the parable of *The Good Samaritan,* Jesus chose to address the topic of money.

"...he handed the innkeeper two silver coins, telling him, 'Take care of this man. If his bill runs higher than this, I'll pay you the next time I'm here.'"

And I say that I find it interesting because, quite often, it is money that casts the deciding vote on treatment options.

Oh, yes... the money.

To gauge how people think, try this experiment with the next five folks you meet, and then we'll close this section with some questions you should be asking.

Tell them you've got a friend or family member who's going to be checking into an inpatient rehab facility for the next 30, 60, or 90 days, and see what kind of response you get.

Chances are, four out of five will track along these lines: "Wow, that sounds *really expensive!* What's that going to cost?"

Imagine that.

Here we are in the life-saving business, and all anyone can think about is the money. So, suddenly recovery looks expensive, but shhh– don't talk about the money washed away with a twenty-year gambling addiction.

Or how about in comparison to a decade of lost wages and destroyed relationships that are suffered by an alcoholic and their family, not to mention the cost of the booze week after week, year after year.

Here is a good question that keeps it all in perspective: would you rather invest in an effective recovery program, or pay for a twelve month habit of an actively-using cocaine addict?

Suddenly, rehab– competent, skilled, and experienced rehab– seems like a much less expensive option.

"Now, hang on Shelly," you say, "if rehabs have only a 3% success rate, why even bother?"

Let's be very clear. I said that rehab– by itself– has a 3% success rate for long-term recovery. When used as advocated here in *The Samaritan Solution,* you will find it is dramatically higher!

This is a fact– rehab is nearly 100% effective in stopping the addict from using long enough to begin other treatment.

Nearly 100%.

And this is essential, because we *cannot* treat a using addict.

So, if Mom is fighting diabetes and high blood pressure as a result of her food addiction and she just can't seem to quit eating what's killing her, rehab will make her stop.

Joe's smoking and Barbara's gambling are done, if they're in rehab. And Uncle Curt won't be showing up at the next birthday party drunk. In fact, he won't be there at all– thank goodness, he'll be in rehab!

And amazingly, very little drinking goes on there!

So when it comes to the rehab centers, there is only one common denominator that matters.

Do they get results?

Period.

That's right– do they work to arrest the user from using?

And here's a flash: there is a big difference between those organizations that *say* they can help you, and those that *really* can.

So let me give you a few other questions to ask when you're considering a rehab for a friend or family member– you know, beyond just, "How much is this thing going to cost?"

1) How is the facility equipped to offer detox services under the direction of qualified medical staff? The effects of withdrawal can not only be difficult– without proper medical oversight they can be deadly. At the same time, rehabilitation and counseling therapy cannot be accomplished with someone who is still using.

2) How is the family included in the program? The best facilities recognize, include and treat the entire family as the identified patient. It is not enough just to educate those in the environment about addiction– in many cases, they helped shape the addictive environment to begin with.

3) To what degree are psychiatric professionals part of the treatment team? Often, there are underlying psycho and psycho-social components to addiction, which must be treated if the patient is to experience lasting recovery.

4) How are the residential facilities customized to properly accommodate the specific requirements of your loved one's treatment needs? Addiction recovery seldom allows a one-size-fits-all approach. An environment that is too lenient for some would be too restrictive for others.

5) What is the average length of the inpatient or residential stay at the facility, and what is the relapse rate among those treated? As a rule, the shorter the stay, the greater the chance of relapse. Choose wisely– it may be difficult to get the patient into a future program if they relapse on this one.

6) How are Twelve Step fellowships incorporated into the treatment program? Based on the founding Principles, Steps and Traditions of Alcoholics Anonymous, all Twelve Step fellowships have the effect of providing unconditional love and acceptance in an environment that promotes personal and spiritual growth and accountability.

7) What is the process for aftercare and follow-up? The most successful treatment and rehab centers understand the importance of counseling to teach the critical life skills necessary to re-enter society as a productive, functioning, and responsible individual.

Now, I know you're still chomping at the bit to find out how much it's going to cost. Of course, that's reasonable, so go ahead and ask away.

And while you're at it, see what portion your insurance might cover and whether or not there are state or federal programs that may help defray the cost. Also, some facilities offer financing arrangements to take some of the sting out of the price tag as well.

And one last thing. We've been together long enough now that you know that the cost of doing nothing will far outweigh the cost of successful treatment.

However, as the leader, as the Samaritan, you will need to stand vigilant– because often, doing nothing is the route that the others around you will want to choose to go.

Of course, that doesn't cost them a dime. But it may come at the cost of your loved one's life.

COUNT TO TWELVE

Okay, so what do the following sets of letters have in common?

AA, AAA, CA, CMA, COSLAA, FA, FAA, GA, MA, NA, NicA, OA, OLGA, SA, another SA, SAA, SCA, SLAA, and WA.

Well, if you said there's a whole lot of A's in there, you'd be correct! And the similarities don't stop there.

Each one of these organizations is based on the principles of Alcoholics Anonymous (AA), and each exists in one form or another as a fellowship of men and women who come together to offer their experience, strength, and hope to others who desire to stop using whatever it is they are using.

Of the list above, one is for the support of those suffering from an addiction to alcohol, one is for *all* addictions, four for drug addicts, three for those with food addictions, two for gamblers, five for those with sexual addictions, two for smokers, and one for workaholics.

Oh, and we also have Co-Anon, CoDA, COSA, another FA, Al-Anon/Alateen, Gam-Anon/Gam-A-Teen and Nar-Anon for the families and friends who are suffering right along as a result of their loved one's addiction.

Clearly, there is a need for support among those who are suffering from the devastating effects of addiction in this country, and we are thankful that these groups exist.

Unfortunately, even with the Open Source wiki-culture of the Internet, there is still too much misinformation about these organizations and the benefits they offer.

Many who could benefit know nothing about them.

Indeed, in the mid-90's, at the very point that my wife's food addiction was about to manifest into the cancer that would steal her life, there was a Twelve Step meeting for a food addiction group that gathered just several blocks away– a group that we never knew existed, until it was too late.

Please hear what I'm going to say next.

As addicts, and families of addicts, we know two things:

1) We cannot overcome addiction alone, and

2) We have a responsibility to help others who cannot do it by themselves either.

In between those two statements you'll find a templated Twelve Step process and the support of many others who have walked in your shoes and who are willing to share your journey to lasting peace and recovery.

There is help for you right now, Believer– for your family, for your friend, and for your loved one– through Twelve Step fellowships that are likely meeting within thirty minutes of your home.

And, if not, you can start a group of your own.

After all, you're a leader.

Now, here's what else you need to know:

Twelve Step programs, by themselves, have limitations.

Remember our 3% success figure?

It is the same here. As singular programs to achieve complete abstinence and recovery, they hover right around 3%.

"But no, no, no, Shelly!! My friend Thomas goes to Twelve Step meetings a couple times a week and he is soberrrrrrr..."

You can stop there.

We've been through this– and the numbers, are the numbers.

Yes, I understand that your friend, Thomas, has quit drinking. And I also see that he is very unhealthy, overweight and smoking like he's on fire. Thomas is dry– he is not sober.

Just recently, I had the opportunity to speak with a handful of individuals who have been on the road to addiction recovery for many years.

Each spoke of the relationships that had been damaged, the hurt they had caused, the struggle to keep their thoughts from drifting toward the guilt and shame that seemed to rear up and wear them down every so often.

And they spoke of the anger and loneliness that they still felt so frequently.

I listened intently, and then asked the $64,000 question:

"How long has it been since you last used?"

Several puffed out their chests immediately. Eleven years, sixteen years, twenty-one years.

Others were more quiet. More reserved.

A couple of months, three and a half weeks, seventeen hours.

Several questions entered my mind:

First, regarding the initial respondents– the three with the forty-eight years' combined sobriety– why are they still experiencing such trouble in their lives and relationships?

Why do they look so unhealthy, and why are their

relationships at home and at work on such a razor's edge?

After all, if they were *really* sober, shouldn't these problems have resolved long ago?

This is a difficult reality to face– the fact that they weren't really sober at all but had merely traded their addiction to alcohol or drugs for an addiction to smoking or food or something else.

And then were the questions with regard to the second group. These are men and women who have been around the block, and then some. Men and women who know the pitfalls and the triggers. If anyone could avoid a slip or relapse, shouldn't it be them?

Well, yes... maybe.

But it seems that when speaking about recovery, living *with* addiction is the easiest thing you can do. On the other hand, living clean– living with *sobriety*– now, that's the hard part.

I lay this out because of the pesky money issue that often crops up in family discussions about what to do next. You see, compared to rehab, and in contrast to counseling, Twelve Step programs cost, well... virtually nothing.

And that is likely to be attractive to some of those in your circle of friends or family.

You need to stand tall.

You need to lead.

Yes, as a one-third part of the recovery plan, these programs add up to success for you and your loved one.

However, alone, they are found wanting.

So, how about the final component– the third leg of the recovery stool? And what difference will it really make?

THE WHOLE IS GREATER
THAN THE SUM OF ITS PARTS

So, I'd imagine by now you have at least a few questions, especially after reading the last two sections of this chapter.

Specifically, if proper medical intervention– rehab– yields a successful recovery rate of only about 3% when pursued as a standalone strategy, and if Twelve Step programs fare about the same, where is the hope for you and your family now?

Further, what if you've already been down those trails a time or two and the very notion of dredging up all the hurt once again leaves you feeling sick in the pit of your stomach?

Well, thank goodness, there is still counseling!

"Oh c'mon, now, Shelly!" someone says.

Yes?

"Let's be serious. I know you're a counselor and all, but you can't tell me that counseling alone is suddenly going to handle all of this! I mean, you *just said* that rehab can't do it, for Pete's sake! And the Twelve Steps, well, they were custom-made for situations like this!!"

Yes, and your point?

Now, let me be very clear about this:

As a counselor, I understand that some will expect me to say that counseling, or therapy as it is also known, is addiction's magic bullet– the miracle cure for the most common and deadly disease in the country.

Yes, and having been long down that road myself, having been the beneficiary of some really bad therapy by some grossly incompetent counselors over the years, I understand the skepticism.

So, believe me when I tell you that I understand completely the preposterous nature of what I am about to say next.

If you get the right counselor– a man or woman who really knows their stuff– and if the addict agrees to see that counselor one-on-one, without the family, without the aid of the other two legs of the stool, the success results will climb all the way... to about 3%.

"Oh my, what a compelling plug for your services," you say.

And you are right. But in this day and age of wild claims and untested programs and outright scams, you must know the truth. You cannot fall prey to the fancy pitches and the slick advertising.

And you cannot pick and choose your treatment options as if this were an *à la carte* menu posted in the window of your favorite restaurant downtown.

Such an approach guarantees only one result. Without a plan, you will sail headlong into a financial and emotional meltdown.

Yes, I know there are operators out there, hucksters who will sell you whatever you are willing to buy and take whatever money you are willing to spend. And I really believe that they should be locked up and the key tossed into a landfill.

However, you need a plan right this very minute that will work and that you can get started with immediately, so here it is. Write this down, copy it off and paste it to your refrigerator and bathroom mirror. Take it to your next family meeting, and present your decision, with love.

It's *The Samaritan Solution* recovery formula for success!

Proper medical intervention
Twelve Step fellowship program(s)
Individual, group, and family counseling
+ Lifetime commitment
= 96% recovery rate for you and your loved one

And,of course, that raises questions.

Is it really possible to see success rates that high?

What's really involved in counseling anyway?

Why is it so important? How can it be that powerful?

And just how does a family manage all this?

WALKING TOGETHER

A military commander once said that in war, the battle plan works well until the first shot is fired— then all hell breaks loose. At that point, you better have a veteran in the foxhole with you.

He might as well have been talking about addiction.

On second thought, he might as well have been talking about *The Samaritan Solution*. Addiction recovery is full of circumstances and setbacks that are *really not* that difficult, except for one intensely powerful fact: it is your family member or friend who could die if mistakes are made and the process blows up.

This emotional drain on the loved one's family can be nearly unbearable at times, and if you are to succeed, you will need someone to guide you through the minefield.

As we celebrate each new day of sobriety, we also recognize that very *small* events and circumstances can have very *large* negative consequences where this disease is involved, and the choices and options are not always obvious when your point of view is clouded by the smoke from the battlefield.

A trusted counselor can make all the difference at those moments when emotions would otherwise likely get the best of us.

In the next chapter we'll discuss some of the common responsibilities that you as family or friends may be asked to take on, as well as some of the victories and challenges that you may experience and come to expect in recovery.

Regardless, you will find that walking together with those who have gone through it a few thousand times brings stability and confidence to the process that is absolutely invaluable to keeping the rest of your life from falling through the cracks– or falling apart.

From the position of the counselor, the treatment plan will be created, and the resources organized. The family will be strengthened and their roles defined. Arrangements will be made with the proper medical professionals, and aftercare activities and schedules will be coordinated.

Together, we will find and use whatever leverage is available and necessary to get your loved one into the *last* treatment program that they will ever need.

And we will have done it using *The Samaritan Solution* to buy back their life, once and for all.

Part IV:
The Road Home

"Going over to him, the Samaritan soothed his wounds...
and bandaged them."

Chapter 8

*   *   *

Great Expectations

Peace.

Yes, peace and quiet.

The first *real* peace you've felt for what seems to be ages. On second thought, it has been ages, literally years, since you felt this confident about the future– since you felt your friend or family member was safe.

For a family who has been struggling with addiction, no moment may be more peaceful, more memorable, than the one that takes place the morning after their loved one begins rehabilitation in a competent facility.

Lying in bed, knowing that– for the first time in a long time– their friend or loved one is not using, not self-destructing.

Confident that they're receiving the medical attention that will remove the threat from this day.

Yes, today, there will be no arguments.

Today, no panicked telephone calls.

Today, no further damage to themselves or others.

Today.

And maybe, just for today, you should bask in the moment, enjoy a light lunch and coffee with friends. Soak in the tub, spend some time in devotions, or an hour with a good book. Maybe you could even take in a movie with your spouse, walk the mall, or get a massage. And then, let's talk– because tomorrow, the real work of recovery begins.

Whether you realize it or not, you've likely just set out on what may be the most important journey of your life. Indeed, it may be the reason for your life here on earth. And, though it may not yet be apparent, you are on your way to following Jesus' teaching– and becoming a hero.

Certainly, to the friend or family member who has just begun treatment, your actions, your involvement, may have spared their very life. And your next moves will likely go a long way to determining the final outcome.

Congratulations– you're loving your neighbor.

Yes, this is the work of a Samaritan. And you must be vigilant, you must stay strong. Because, at times, the path to recovery can seem to be as rough as the road to addiction that came before.

But take heart!

Recovery and restoration are coming, and help is near.

In fact, that last statement, "help is near," may be one of the greatest gifts you'll ever receive. You see, it's true that you can choose to keep all of this to yourself.

Yes, you can try to ride this storm alone.

But you don't have to.

And surely, that is not the model that we were given!

By now it is obvious that once the Samaritan in our story recognized trouble, he did not waver nor did he collapse. Feeling compassion for his fellow man, he followed both his instincts and his heart to do what he knew how to do– apparently some basic first aid– and then immediately got the victim to a place of safety and security and healing where he organized help from others.

That's it... *The Samaritan Solution.*

The model for loving God– by loving our neighbor– is really that simple.

Do what you can, and then get help from others. In effect, the Good Samaritan of our story simply put together a team approach to recovery for the victim.

And that is exactly what I will help *you* to do also.

Please understand, addiction recovery is a customized process, and no two are exactly alike. So while it's true that you must go in with your eyes open, and yes, you must stay prepared to lead, it doesn't always require a Herculean effort on your part.

In fact, I have seen many instances where the hero of the family did nothing more than make a few phone calls and connections on the front end, and that was enough.

On the other hand, I have seen others who were very involved in all phases and every detail of the recovery.

What is necessary is a genuine commitment to the process. And I want you to know that regardless of how recovery plays out with your loved one, you may be assured of these two things:

First, there are extraordinarily competent and caring individuals who are willing to walk with you every step of the way.

And second, you can learn to recognize and completely avoid the most common challenges and biggest obstacles to recovery.

ANNIVERSARIES GREAT AND SMALL

Some days are truly unforgettable.

In fact, they can define a mission, a career, or a lifetime.

From time to time I think of the four years that I invested with my practice in the Midwest, and the truly wonderful people that I met. Of all the time that I was there, one late summer morning will stay with me always– a day that absolutely defines the goodness that happens when all the pieces of recovery come together.

Up before daybreak, I planned my route and prepared my remarks. The drive would take me on an hour and a half road trip through the rustic north woods, flowing family farms, and old logging towns.

It was beautiful. Just like the postcards.

At mid-morning on a Sunday, there was little traffic as I wound my way past state parks and scenic river-ways, on a mission to meet old friends. Oh, and the weather was perfect– not something that can be counted on at that time of year in Wisconsin and Upper Michigan.

Indeed, there is an old saying in that part of the Midwest that it matters little if you like the weather or not... just wait a little while, and it will change. Some days with a vengeance, and other days, to perfection!

No doubt, this was a *perfection* day.

And what an occasion!

Anniversaries are common– sixty-year anniversaries are not!

In fact, this was only the seventh such event that I've attended in my entire lifetime. You see, we're not speaking of a 60th wedding anniversary, though those can be fairly rare also. And we're not speaking of the 60th anniversary of the founding of a church or a business either.

No, we are speaking of a dear friend's 60th anniversary of sobriety.

Now, let me state very clearly what I *did not* just say.

I *did not* just say that sobriety was a rare event.

In fact, as has been previously noted, during the past forty years or so, I have personally helped over nine thousand people in my practice become sober from their drug or activity of choice. I have also witnessed– at a distance– the recovery of thousands more outside of my practice.

That's all well and good.

However, when it comes to numbers like sixty-years' sobriety, the math simply works against alcoholics and addicts of every sort.

For example, if a person begins their journey in their mid-thirties or forties– which is a very common event– well, you don't need a calculator to figure out when they will celebrate their 60th anniversary.

And sixty years is an incredible accomplishment for other reasons, as well. You see, the decision to stop using, yes, the act of quitting, is only the first step. Many former users live lives in which they are surrounded by all of the reasons they used in the first place.

Same people, same stresses, same triggers.

And after spending what could amount to a small fortune on a successful rehab, a rehab in which the user really ceases using, the addict goes back to living in an environment that encourages them to slide into their former lifestyle.

It's important to understand this, for it could very quickly steal all the joy you were feeling as you soaked in the tub at the beginning of this chapter!

Please know that since you made the commitment to get involved, your dream of seeing your loved one celebrate long-term anniversaries is now well within the realm of possibility, though it may mean changing up the environment in which they live.

To clarify, here's an example from someone who's struggling.

I happened to run into an old acquaintance recently who has battled food addiction for years. I had never met her husband before, and it was a pleasure to finally put a face with his name, and also to connect a few dots.

You see, throughout the years we have known each other, our

conversations often revolved around issues of addiction and recovery. Particularly, the circumstances regarding her vicious cycle of abstinence and relapse.

Periodically, as we'd see each other, she'd ask how long it had been for me, and then mention that she currently had three weeks on a program. Yes, she said, she was celebrating "little" anniversaries, three weeks at a time.

Unfortunately, she was also ruining her health in the process.

Three weeks on, a few weeks off. Three weeks on, a few months off. Three weeks on...

Over and over and over again, for years.

Now, it's no surprise that when you work in the field of addiction, you tend to run into a lot of people whose lives are turned upside down by the disease, and who struggle daily with maintaining their sobriety. But for some, that hill is significantly steeper than others, and it is made so by the environment in which they live.

By the *people* with whom they live.

Such was the case with my friend.

Yes, at the moment, she is once again abstinent. However, her husband– easily carrying an extra hundred pounds or so– clearly is not. And the stress of that relationship and the temptation of living with all those unhealthy products in the cupboard has obviously been– at least to this point– too much for her to bear.

So, she tries hard and succeeds for a time, and then she slips.

Such roller coaster rides– up and down, success and failure, abstinence and relapse– create havoc on our loved one's systems.

Physically as well as emotionally.

The question is, how far are we willing to go to save the life of another? To stack the odds in favor of recovery?

In our story, it was the hero's choice also, and, no doubt, it is the very foundation of *The Samaritan Solution.*

Each morning in America, both ourselves and our loved ones are surrounded by all of the substances, commodities, and opportunities that could end our sobriety that day. We are bombarded by advertising and entertainment that promote an addictive culture, and by industries that prosper even as we succumb.

By now we are all too well aware that the struggle is similar regardless of the addiction. With the exception of illicit street drugs, most of our vices are perfectly legal, and their promoters are taxpaying business men and women who are just responding to societal demands.

Yes, addicts and their families make for a very predictable and reliable target market!

Individuals who are struggling with addictions tend to be pretty good consumers– and their next fix is as close as the grocery store or doctor's office, the casino or gas station, the mall or the Internet or the kitchen counter.

When viewed from this perspective, it is easy to understand relapse. Staying sober and healthy, "One Day At A Time," is not so simple when we live those 24 hours in an addictive environment.

You have often heard me say that your loved one's recovery begins the moment *you* decide to be committed, to get involved. And that is a commitment and involvement that is ongoing.

"Wait, Shelly– you're saying that..."

Yes, I am saying that to a great degree, the very success or failure of your loved one's recovery is influenced by your commitment and involvement. And therein lies the challenge.

Not only are most family members at a loss on how and where to begin, but they may not want to change their own habits and behaviors that could be contributing to the continuance of the addiction and the hindrance of recovery.

THE TRUE PRICE OF RECOVERY

This is the heart of the matter– and it calls for a leader.

We've seen that the Samaritan seemingly had *no issues* to think over. His decisions were already made, settled by the depth of his character.

As the story unfolds, he would do whatever he could do, and then he would enlist help for the rest. Yes, he would be responsible for paying the price of the victim's recovery, even the recovery of a complete stranger– the recovery of his enemy– his neighbor.

"Then he put the man on his own donkey and took him to an inn, where he took care of him. The next day he handed the innkeeper two silver coins, telling him, 'Take care of this man. If his bill runs higher than this, I'll pay you the next time I'm here.'"

The question is, are we prepared to pay whatever price we need to pay, to learn whatever we need to learn, to change the environment that we live in and give our loved one the greatest opportunity for success?

And now here is the truth– most families are not.

Let me repeat: most families are not.

And it's not that the price tag is too high in terms of finances. No, that they are usually willing to pay. I have often seen families pull together and contribute thousands and even tens of thousands of dollars to the recovery effort, and then fall down on the most critical aspects of long-term success.

Please accept this with the love in which it is offered, because mistakes now could wipe out all the good that you and your family have done up until this point.

Let's look at where the resistance comes from, because these are issues that you may face during the course of your loved one's recovery– if not from yourself personally, then from others in the circle of family or friends.

In the earliest stages of recovery, one of the first and most difficult principles for families and friends is that we cannot do therapy or counseling with an addict who is still using.

Earlier, I mentioned that many families are so on edge– either totally frustrated or in extreme despair– that when we initially meet they just want to unload their family member onto someone else's shoulders and into someone else's care.

They just want the situation, and their loved one, handled.

"We'll pay you anything! We're at the end of our rope! We don't even care what you do– just help us!"

And often, the families are shocked when I tell them that I don't want to meet with the addict right now– instead, I need to meet with *them*.

In virtually every home where addiction lives, the damage has been building for years, and is so extensive that the individuals themselves don't know the extent of the hurt they have received– or that they have caused. Yes, caused.

Very often, over time, *the family* has made things worse.

Sometimes, much worse.

I can say this to you, and I know you will accept it in the manner given, because by now you know my heart, and I know a little of yours as well. You wouldn't have read this far if you didn't have the makings of a Good Samaritan.

You see, it is possible that the entire family may need counseling if they are to create valuable life-strategies and thought-habits that will serve them well.

And suddenly, commitment can begin to break down.

"Wait a minute, Shelly," a family member says. "Are you saying the rest of us have to take part in these activities? I mean, we got brother Kyle to go to rehab, and I know he's planning to go to a Twelve Step and counseling when he's out, but I certainly don't need any help– there's nothing wrong with me!"

You *may* be right.

But let's look at what I'm suggesting... and what I'm *not*.

I believe that in order to fully achieve the level of success that *The Samaritan Solution* advocates– up to a 96% recovery rate– the entire family (and friends, if necessary) must be ready, willing, and available to take part in all three phases of treatment:

1) Proper medical intervention,
2) Twelve Step fellowship, and
3) Individual, group and family counseling.

Again, you should be *ready, willing, and available.*

I *did not* say it was required for recovery in every case.

But over time, addiction harms all relationships, and causes both the addict and those close by to begin to act in dysfunctional ways. Without correction, the environment will usually lead the addict right back into the aberrant behavior. Worse, it nearly always affects others within the family system as well.

It is typically most evident as it spreads into the next generation– the children, grandchildren, or the nieces or nephews of the addict. At the very least, it is my conviction that we owe it to the innocents to raise them in a safe and functional home.

After all, *any* Samaritan could tell us that!

Also, before we tell ourselves that *we're* all doing just fine, let's not stray too far from the numbers.

With tens of millions of Americans suffering from one addiction or another, from those who can't live without their cigarettes or alcohol to those caught up in the widespread use of pharmaceuticals and pornography, and the two out of every three homes in the country within which someone is suffering from the effects of food addiction, the environment for relapse is primed and loaded.

It's not difficult to see that Dad's drinking, sister Jean's obesity, or Mom's shopping are just as likely to throw Bobby into a tailspin from his crack rehab as any of his other relationships.

So, let me ask once more: are you willing to pay the price of recovery for your loved one, even if it includes seeking help and support for yourself?

We began the chapter by painting a beautiful picture of the peace, tranquility, and feeling of security that accompany medical intervention. Anybody who has ever felt helpless as a loved one slowly self-destructed knows the feeling of confidence and release that is inspired when their friend or family member is suddenly safe.

As important as great medical intervention is, however, please keep these thoughts in mind:

1) Assuming your loved one actually goes to rehab, they will likely be inpatient in a perfectly clean, controlled, and temptation-free environment for 90 days or so, clinically supervised by extraordinary teams of professionals,

2) Upon their release, they will live the remainder of their life in the temptation-rich world and whatever home environment that you and your family and friends create together, and

3) Rehab, by itself, delivers only a 3% success rate.

But don't misunderstand– rehab accomplishes what neither the addict, nor you, nor I can accomplish: at least for the time that they're inpatient, they will not be using.

And the withdrawal, which can be downright nasty to the degree that it would destroy most families, is completely supervised by competent medical teams.

Yes, it's a thing of beauty.

Over the course of a few months, effective rehab wipes the slate clean, detoxifies the body, and prepares the individual for the next phase.

And that is why I am so strong on aftercare, strengthening the family, and building a vibrant environment where recovery continues and the patient thrives. Without you– and a solid recovery plan– your loved one has a 97% chance of using again, and that is certainly not the goal.

So, let's look at a few normal situations that we all encounter, situations that can steal the sobriety of your loved one and throw your entire family back into confusion.

And then we'll walk together through some solutions that you can use along the way.

Let me ask you this: how could such routine things as air travel, a church potluck, or a short hospital stay threaten sobriety?

You see, that is what we are up against in dealing with addiction. Activities that are absolutely fine for others, that no one else gives a second thought, *aren't* necessarily fine for us.

In fact, without proper planning, it is not uncommon that travel for vacations or business, simple get-togethers for fun or fellowship, or a minor injury or illness could end one's abstinence and send their behavior and addiction into a spiral that may take years to pull out of once again!

I'll use some examples from the point of view of a food addict, since that is the malady that causes the greatest challenges for the greatest number of people, and then we'll establish some guides to avoid such temptations.

It isn't surprising that food addicts have an especially difficult road to travel. With all other addictions, the goal is simple abstinence– a smoker must quit smoking and a gambler must quit gambling. But food is another story.

We can't just *quit* eating.

Yet, we must not eat trigger foods, and for most of us that means giving up products that contain sugar, flour, and wheat.

Try that with your next airline flight, congregational bake sale, or visit to the hospital. That's right– they actually have a generous selection of unhealthy food at the hospital!

Imagine that!

But here's what's important to remember: the addict not only *wants* to use, the addict also *needs* to use, and they are actively searching for excuses to do just that.

Sadly, such normal life experiences can provide the cover that allows the addict to use again and rationalize it in the process.

If you only take one thing from this section, take this.

Any excuse will work for an addict who is looking to use, so get ready for statements like:

"Well, the flight attendant offered the soda and chips and I didn't want to appear rude." Or, "The convention went through all the trouble to cater the meal, and I didn't want to seem ungrateful."

How about this gem: "It would have been a shame to waste all the food at the church. After all, everyone worked so hard. Besides, it was only one– okay, it was only two– pieces of cake. I can quit again tomorrow."

Or the pinnacle of rationalization: "The nurse brought me the fruit juice and the Popsicle. How bad could it be? My doctor doesn't seem to have a problem with all that sugar, so why should I?"

Well, if you or a loved one is a food addict, here's one good reason to be concerned: that addiction is going to steal the best days of the best months of the best years of your life, and replace them with illness and disease and an early death.

But just knowing that is not enough.

You see, it isn't sufficient to simply teach this knowledge– we must also teach its practical application. That is why Part IV is so aptly titled, "The Road Home."

You must know what life is going to look like in recovery, both good and bad, and you must make sure to have a *Plan B* if and when *Plan A* runs into trouble.

I want to share with you that, recently, I was able to traverse each of these kinds of activities while still keeping my winning abstinence streak intact– and so can you.

It isn't difficult, but it does require knowledge and planning.

As we spoke of previously, the recovery rates in this country are abysmally low, and a great deal of that is because of lousy aftercare and follow-up.

But the truth is, even if the rates all across the nation hovered at the 96% that we see in our practice, that would still not be good enough, because I believe it should literally be 100% of the cases.

Complete success requires just two things:

1) Getting on a program, and
2) Staying on the program.

Of the two, which one is easier? Getting on, or staying on?

Kind of a silly question, isn't it? Even the people who deny the existence of food addiction get this one right. For without proper help and support, staying on the program can be exceedingly difficult.

Ready for another question?

This one is only for that group of deniers mentioned above. If food addiction doesn't exist, if these substances aren't addictive, then why is it so hard to give them up?

Try completely going off all sugar, flour, and wheat products for the next seven days and call me if you find it troublesome.

Yes, call me when you begin to experience withdrawal, when your body aches and when you get irritable as all get-out.

I'll be waiting by the phone.

Thankfully, though, there is hope and there is recovery.

Staying on the program is not only possible, but it is also possible *every time.* It requires detailed planning to eliminate temptation, and to ensure that the proper food choices are available when and where you need them.

Of course, therein lies part of the issue, because we know that addicts look for opportunities to use. That upcoming trip out of town? Why, that's a great chance to binge when no one is looking.

The church potluck for Harry and Norma's fiftieth wedding anniversary? Well, that provides the perfect cover to partake of the piles of pasta, cake, and ice cream that are slowly and surely raising congregational blood sugar levels to the height of the church steeple.

And that visit to the local medical center? This is touchy, but having recently had a one week stay for a hernia operation, I can tell you the two common denominators that exist for over 80% of the patients *and* staff: they all eat too much lousy food and get too little exercise.

And coming or going, it shows.

Maintaining abstinence from the sugar, flour and wheat

products that are spiking and crashing your blood sugar and insulin levels is not always easy, but it does not have to be impossible either.

It begins with a decision, and the commitment to stay clean. And that commitment is followed by action. Arrangements must be made to avoid those substances, and that means being proactive.

Here are some tips to stay abstinent yourself, or to help your loved one overcome these specific challenges:

When traveling, especially by air, explain to the TSA agents that you are on a very restricted diet due to "severe food allergies." Seldom will they argue this, and you won't have to educate them about addiction. Bring your own food in small packages that meet the regulations, and plan to shop immediately upon arrival at your destination.

Oh, and do everyone a favor and arrive at the airport early in the event that the officers want to take extra time to look at all your healthy meal items.

What about that next potluck at the church? Team up with another individual or two, and bring abstinent-friendly food. It is the only way to guarantee that there will actually *be* healthy food at the event– but take heart, because experience shows that very few people go for the nutritious choices, so you'll not only have enough, but there will almost certainly be leftovers to bring home.

Don't believe me?

You be the judge at the next luncheon.

And how about the trip to the hospital? Well, this takes a little more commitment, because you are challenging the system– but you must. Ask your nurse to arrange a meeting with the staff nutritionist and chef– yes, they will do this for you, but only if you ask.

Then, explain that you have allergies to sugar, flour, and wheat, and let them help solve the problem.

It works, and I've found they're glad to do it.

And my continued abstinence streak is proof.

What's important from this point forward is to do whatever is necessary to keep yourself or your loved one protected the next time circumstances present the opportunity to slip.

These are some of the routine challenges that a good counselor can help you to overcome with excellence.

Let's look at a few more.

HAPPY HOLIDAYS

It's a phrase that has recently come to symbolize one time of the year here in America.

Yes, the season which for decades, even centuries, was known by the familiar greetings of Happy Hanukkah and Merry Christmas has now been sanitized by whoever is in charge of sanitizing such things.

But my problem isn't with the political correctness of the phrase.

No, I just happen to know how many other holidays there are that can cause a real problem with addiction.

You need to know this, Believer– holidays are a time for real vigilance on your part.

Evenly spaced and sprinkled throughout the year– by acts of Congress no less– are major and minor holidays, which virtually ensure that the fine folks who work at greeting card companies the world over will always have a chicken in the pot.

However, as a family that has struggled through addiction, you know the pain and stress of past holidays, and you look forward with hope to a time of real restoration in the future.

First, I want you to know that millions of others share your feelings. Stress and trepidation around holidays and family gatherings is fairly common– because addiction is fairly common.

When consulting, Steve often advises others not to make *big* decisions on *bad* days. And that is especially good advice as you get together with family and friends throughout the year.

You see, I know you just want the addiction to go away, I know you want an end to the volatile behavior, and I know you paid for the rehab and wish it would all be behind you by now. But some of these issues are very deep.

When families spend as much time together as they do on holidays, it can lead to tensions– however, if you add addiction to the mix, you've got the potential for some real fireworks.

There is little doubt as to why you need to prepare for the battle. After all, you already know that this may constitute the greatest fight of your life, a fight in which there is little room for error.

But when we think of holidays and the pressure that comes with them, I also want to share another perspective.

I want you to look at the disease of addiction from the point of view of its victim.

I want you to put yourself in the shoes of one wracked with guilt and shame over the lies and the letdowns, the anger and the arguments, the temptations and tirades and tempers.

I want you to feel the fear and the failure, the pain and embarrassment, the loss of self and sanity.

Please understand that your loved one never wanted things to turn out this way. *No one* wants to turn out this way. And though they are perfectly willing to crush you, they really never wanted to hurt you.

And, while we're at it, they also don't want cirrhosis, and they don't want cancer, nor do they want diabetes and high blood pressure and heart disease.

They don't want to cough anymore, and they don't want the test results that are waiting for them on Monday morning.

And, more than likely, they don't want you and everyone else to see them. Not right now, and not like this.

Getting together with family, friends, or acquaintances at the church or synagogue only reinforces their grave condition– reminding them of all that is missing and broken and hurting.

And though they may have recently stopped using, though they successfully made it through the rehab phase, they still possess all the memories and negative emotions from all those years of *Unhappy Holidays*.

This is also true for other family events– birthdays, weddings, and funerals.

Finally, you need to be aware of one other issue.

There is conflicting research that states that the biggest spike of the year for suicides among addicts happens around holiday events. The idea is that this is when they are at their lowest point– feeling the least capable, the least competent, and the least worthy.

Whether that is true or not, this is as good a time as any to be watchful for your loved one. Though it may be difficult at times, your holidays *can* be joyful once again... if you walk those roads together.

FEELING STRONG

We've just invested a significant amount of time discussing realistic expectations for your loved one's recovery, and for your own commitment and involvement.

You understand that if the situation is to improve, there may be times that you need to lead.

You also know that it is possible that you may face opposition from both the addict and other family members and friends, that the recovery will likely be both exhilarating and demanding, and that it can require that you make and model permanent lifestyle changes yourself.

And I believe that there is no greater purpose for your life!

We have also spoken quite extensively about the mental and emotional strains that can set the stage for the relapse of your loved one back into the craziness, back into self-destruction and depression, back into addiction.

But not all of the triggers are on the emotional or relational planes. Some may be purely physical.

Before we leave this chapter, I would like to give you some advice for when those situations arise. I believe these suggestions are both simple *and* revolutionary.

You see, even after successful rehab, even with the support that you and your friend or family member will receive through Twelve Step programs and counseling, even after the excruciating pain of withdrawal begins to fade into memory, physical triggers can abound.

If proper rest or nutrition are lacking, these physical triggers combine with the emotional and relational components in a sort of snowball effect that can be overwhelming to your loved one.

But it needn't be so.

A personal story, and a message of hope:

It could have been any Saturday, I suppose. I was up at 5:15 A.M., and raring to go within an hour, the same as virtually every other day of the week. And while I know that there are some who would prefer to sleep in on weekends– or, for that matter, go to bed early– I just can't do it.

Call it passion, call it a mission, but there are simply too many things to do, and far too many people to help. And nothing gets done lounging in bed, or sitting by the pool sipping iced tea.

Now, don't get me wrong.

I didn't say that I don't enjoy the pool. In fact, a daily swim is one of the reasons I'm up every morning before dawn. And I like iced tea, though it has now generally been replaced by ultra-nutritious smoothies– but more on that in a moment.

Yes, exercise and healthy nutrition are essential to sober living, a necessary and intentional part of every day. But back to my story, because this wasn't just any weekend morning. No, this particular Saturday was, well, a particularly special day!

You see, it was a celebration for me, one of those anniversaries of which we spoke earlier. Actually, the truth is that it was a public recognition of the forty-one years of sobriety that I had achieved on September 10th, right in the middle of my move a few years ago to beautiful South Florida.

Yes, more than four decades of clean living, having literally come back from death's door.

And all this I say, not to be overly dramatic, but to let you know that a great life is available to you and your loved one once again. After all, I was given just six months to live... in 1968.

It is interesting that after all this time, the people who should be *in the know* are still very often *in the dark!* And yes, this does tie back to my opening story about rising early, and getting plenty of exercise and proper nutrition.

After all, when we don't feel good about ourselves, we are more at risk to fall backwards. You see, regardless of the type of addiction, we know that certain activities must be maintained, and others avoided, if we are to preserve our sobriety.

We spoke of the need to stay out of environments that promote the substance or behavior to which we are addicted. We know we must change the routines and conduct that are associated with our addiction, and replace them with life-giving actions and relationships that support our recovery.

We're prepared to seek professional help when necessary and form strong bonds and friendships with others who have gone before, those who can share their experience, strength and hope at the time we need it most.

And we are aware of triggers that might cause a relapse, be they substances like alcohol, drugs, tobacco and food, behaviors like gambling and pornography, or the dangerous circumstances of being hungry, angry, lonely and tired.

Yes– once sober, we must stand strong, one day at a time.

But when we focus only on the addiction in front of us, we miss what is going on in the background. As you know, when we attack alcoholism, for example, other temptations and activities begin to pop up. So then we switch gears and do battle over there, only to have a third front open up, or a relapse back to the first.

This is draining on the patient and the family alike, and it is also quite unnecessary. You see, very often, this circle of disaster is helped along by nutritional deficiencies that promote the cravings that become so irresistible. And while it may not win any points with those who make their living in the chemical and pharmaceutical markets, the answer may be as close as your local grocery store or your kitchen counter.

To help alleviate the physical and emotional stress that can come during recovery, I want to introduce you to a nutritional concept that I believe will help you in the event you or someone you love is involved in any form of addiction, or the negative health circumstances associated with it.

And no, I am not creating a Thirteenth Step!

Here is what I have learned:

Packed with vitamin- and mineral-rich fruits and vegetables and nutrient-dense superfoods, green smoothies, nutritional shakes, and products that cleanse the body are a delicious and highly effective way to eliminate cravings and provide a natural shot of extreme nutrition that can help stabilize appetite, mood, self-esteem, and energy.

In short, they can assist in keeping your loved one from getting hungry, angry, lonely, and tired– the very circumstances that have been known to be present just prior to so many relapses.

I can tell you that I have personally witnessed the remarkable results that can accompany a program that has a focus on a healthy diet, along with proper rest and exercise.

And, just as significant, when you are leading and giving so much of yourself to others, it's important for you to feel your very best each and every day.

This process builds strength upon strength, creates wonderful new life-giving habits and thought patterns, and begins to lay a foundation of small and consistent successes on which a whole new healthy and refreshing lifestyle can be established.

Chapter 9

*　　*　　*

Do The Same

Call it the power of duplication.

Or a twenty-eight day program on steroids.

Yes, what would you think if I told you that we could start next Sunday and, in just four weeks, reach out with the hope of recovery to virtually every person in America who is suffering from any addiction-related complications or illness?

Impossible, you say?

Improbable, I'll give you.

But only because we're missing the most important part of the equation. And that, my friend, is you.

Now, I'm sure you've seen all the puzzles and exponential economic growth models before– you know, the penny you doubled for thirty days that makes Bill Gates long for your business model... the piece of paper that is folded fifty times and can now reach the sun... yes, logical things like that.

But the point is, mathematically, they are true.

The practicality, however, is another story.

But here's how it works.

Next Sunday, we meet for coffee and I share the good news of recovery with you. And since this book is now out, I probably give you a copy, along with a link to some online resources and the info where you can find *The Samaritan Solution* in both printed and eBook format for yourself.

Fair enough.

Monday morning, we hit the ground running, but only for ten minutes or so– just long enough for each of us to share the good news of recovery with one individual, and wow... thank you... to share a copy of this book and a link to some online resources.

You get the picture. So, let's review.

Sunday morning, it is just you and me.

Two against the world!

Monday, you contact Sheila, and I meet with Jim– our numbers are four and growing.

Tuesday, we all hit the road, make one contact each, and our four now becomes eight.

Wednesday– well, you see the power. There may be only sixteen of us ready to take on the greatest health problem our nation faces, but several very cool and important things are going on here– not the least of which is that our publisher is getting downright fired up about the book sales!

Sorry... little digression there!

But in all seriousness, the numbers on the team will double every day. And when each one does just a little, no one has to do a lot. Could you and I contact twenty-eight individuals, just one per day for four weeks, to share the hope and plan of recovery? To give them a book and a few resources?

Of course we can– in fact, I do it now almost every day.

Next, could those individuals– you know, Sheila and Jim– contact one person a day for the remainder of the four weeks? Just twenty-seven in all? Clearly, the answer is yes.

And greater numbers mean diminishing work is required. The folks that join the team on the twenty-fifth day, for example, need only to contact three. And those that come on board on day twenty-eight need only to get better themselves.

The work is done.

Four weeks to the day, and our little team has reached 268,435,456 people– wonderful moms and dads and sons and daughters just like our own.

Now, here's the problem with such mathematical models.

I can just hear it now.

Someone is going to come along and say that this could never work because you just can't count on what all those other people are going to do. You can't control them, and they may just haul off and do nothing!

And, of course, they're absolutely right.

We *can't* control what others will do– we can only control what *we're* going to do.

Yes, that is the question that has always been at the very core of *The Samaritan Solution*.

What are *we* going to do?

Recently, I spoke with a minister about the concept of grace. You know, the idea that the Lord offers great blessings and benefits to us that we really don't deserve, or that we've done nothing to earn.

During this interesting discussion, he brought up a story that he said was detailed in a *Boston Globe* article– a wonderful article about an unlikely wedding celebration that took an unexpected turn. As recounted, it happened at the Boston Hyatt Hotel in 1990, and ended with the would-be bride showering the city's homeless with grace.

You see, it seems that her former fiancé had unfortunately come down with a serious case of cold feet, and backed out with little time to spare, leaving her and her family stuck with the facilities rented and no hope for a full refund of the significant deposit that had been made months earlier.

So, what did the heroine of this story decide to do?

She moved ahead with the party! She kept the flower arrangements, brought in the band– and changed the menu selection to "Boneless Chicken" in honor of her former love!

Further, in a move made famous by another 2000 year old parable, found in *Luke 14*, she sent messengers out to the streets– to the homeless shelters and missions– to let them know that they were invited to an incredible celebration.

As reported, for this one very special evening, the palatial hotel was filled with Boston's lowliest citizens: street-people, beggars, and addicts.

All were welcome.

But there was more to the story.

You see, many years earlier, she had also been homeless. She was on the streets, with no future, and yet she had been shown grace. She was able to take advantage of several opportunities, and now– having become successful– she wanted to give back.

She wanted to show grace.

Of course, for believers, the point is that just as the Lord has freely and willingly given to us, so we should freely and willingly give to others– a very valid point, indeed.

And this story was also personal as well.

Quite similarly, many years ago, I was the one who was down and out, sick and overweight, crippled and dying. I was the one abusing alcohol and drugs, along with the people in my relationships.

At one of my lowest moments, having been shunned by four medical teams who had given up on me, I was cared for by complete strangers. I was offered a way out– a path to recovery.

And as the minister related the wedding story, my mind absolutely soared. Drifting back in time to that most important day, September 10th, 1968, the day I began to live again.

The day I received grace.

And from that moment, I have tried to carry this message of hope and recovery to alcoholics and addicts of all kinds, and to share the grace that was given to me those many years ago.

A LIFE OF SIGNIFICANCE

Much has been written, and many courses have been taught over the years, regarding the transition that occurs in a society as its people move from early states of *survival* and *dependance* to finally arriving at a place of *stability* and eventual *success*.

These issues are typically discussed in terms of material considerations. And, in fact, if we took a quick poll and asked the respondents to define these words, chances are that most would give answers that were wrapped in the context of financial or career considerations.

That's not unusual.

Survival and dependance. Well, of course, those refer to the poor in our communities– the unfortunate ones who are down on their luck– jobless, homeless, or worse. In most people's thinking, this is where the addicts live.

As people move up, they hope one day to reside in the great "Middle Class." Yes, stability is the word of the day for these folks. Home ownership, a little cottage somewhere, a couple of cars, a big-screen television, and 2.4 smiling kids in the public school system.

They tend to mind their own business– and occasionally that of their neighbors– and while they may never be wealthy, they tell themselves that at least they're safe and generally happy.

Next, there are the folks you always hear about, those fortunate few whom so many want to imitate: real high-fliers.

Taking their place in the public spotlights, perched on the pedestals of corporate boards and committees, they are the pride of the community and the envy of the competition. Through a combination of hard work, focused achievement, and the right breaks, these folks have reached the pinnacle of success.

Or have they?

You see, beyond the climb from survival and dependance, past the point of stability or the tireless efforts required to achieve financial success, there exists a higher level.

It's a place that is simultaneously open to all, yet reserved only for those who are willing to give away their hearts. This is a place of sacrifice– a destination that few will reach– an address known as *significance*.

The difference?

Success is all about us: what we can have, what we can do, or what we can be. Yes, success is selfish– it is focused on me. And we've all gotten quite comfortable with that. After all, you only live once!

On the other hand, significance is self*less*: it is a place of giving, about improving the lives of others. And *that* is what we are called to do.

Interestingly, these concepts each have a very special meaning for individuals and families who are struggling with the effects of addiction.

In terms of recovery, we can all agree that survival and dependance are very dangerous places to live. At that point, the goal is just to stop using. Period.

Or is there more?

You see, regardless of the addiction, the point of cessation is merely the starting point on a journey that will last the remainder of our lives. Quitting is only the very leading edge, the beginning of stability.

Success, however, is another matter completely. It is defined by the long-term sobriety or cleanness that we all seek, and represents a lifetime of complete abstinence from our substance or activity of choice, along with healing and recovery from our illness.

Now, I've got good news and bad news. The bad news is that such a successful recovery can only be measured at the finish line– the end of our walk here on earth. To be successful in terms of recovery means that you were sober– truly sober– to the last day.

However, the good news is that, thankfully, we don't need to wait at all to begin living a life of significance. Regardless of our current situation, notwithstanding the issues of the day or our positions in our careers, we can begin to live significantly today!

We have discovered the truth– and the truth will set us free.

Just as no one would light a candle only to hide it under a bushel, recovering addicts and families of addicts don't bury the answer to addiction. Not only do we take our own recovery seriously, but also the recovery of others.

We know the pain.

We know the trauma and destruction that has been caused to our reputations and our relationships, our health, our finances, and our futures. And if we are to recover– really recover– then we must reach out to our fellow man and woman with a message of encouragement based on our own experience, strength, and hope.

The blessing that is hidden within our own addiction and recovery is manifested in our ability to provide hope and comfort to someone else with theirs.

And by so doing, every recovering addict has the power to serve, the power to support, and the power to save a life. That is a cause which is *very* significant, and demands our answer.

"Now wait, Shelly– are you saying that we *owe* it to others to reach out and help them?"

Well, actually, someone else said that.

THE ELEVENTH COMMANDMENT

There is a lot of fuss made these days about what kids should or shouldn't be exposed to in our nation's public schools.

Of course, in recent years, much argument has taken place over issues like organized prayer, Evolution vs. Creation, and the offenses caused by symbols such as Menorahs, Crosses, Christmas Trees, and Santa Claus. But none of those quite compare to the rage that has been caused by the posting of a handful of rules or ordinances for Godly living– what most of the world affectionately knows as *The Ten Commandments.*

Also called *The Decalogue,* much energy has been exhausted by some who wish to see these laws taken down from school and government properties.

Now, let me say that this was not much of an issue while growing up in Boro Park. In fact, suggesting that they be removed may have led to the questioning of your mental state by the both the Jews *and* the Irish alike!

And understandably so.

After all, I've never really grasped the great controversy behind statements like, "Don't Murder," "Don't Steal," and, "Don't Even Think About Your Neighbor's Wife!"

Granted, that's a loose interpretation– but you get my point.

Now, for all these years, I must say that I've done quite well teaching twenty-two easy-to-understand principles: the Twelve Steps alongside of *The Ten Commandments.*

That is, until a few years ago, when Steve introduced me to what he referred to as *The Eleventh Commandment.*

The Eleventh Commandment.

Now, I must admit, when I first heard that statement I rolled my eyes, assuming that it was just some Protestant addition, or maybe a translation error adding one more thing that we're not supposed to covet!

But there it was, in so many passages and so many places– and it all made perfect sense. Here, in the simplest of language– in five words or less– are messages of love from the Bible:

> *"Love God... love your neighbor." (Old Testament)*
> *"Love one another." (New Testament)*
> *"Love your neighbor as yourself." (Old and New Testament)*

Originally given to Moses and revealed as *Law* in the Old Testament *Book of Leviticus*, it was later acknowledged and taught by Jesus and His disciples in several different contexts, including His teaching about *The Good Samaritan.* Further, it is literally given as an *additional commandment* by Jesus in the *Book of John.*

> *"So now I am giving you a new commandment: Love each other. Just as I have loved you, you should love each other."*

Several minutes ago, you asked whether or not we actually "owe it to others" to reach out to them in their worldly afflictions.

Deep down, I believe that we both already know the answer to that question. Nevertheless, let's take a look at the entire story as Jesus Christ originally laid it out, one more time.

Please read it with me...

One day an expert in religious law stood up to test Jesus by asking him this question: "Teacher, what should I do to inherit eternal life?"

Jesus replied, "What does the law of Moses say? How do you read it?"

The man answered, "'You must love the Lord your God with all your heart, all your soul, all your strength, and all your mind.' And, 'Love your neighbor as yourself.'"

"Right!" Jesus told him. "Do this and you will live!"

The man wanted to justify his actions, so he asked Jesus, "And who is my neighbor?"

Jesus replied with a story: "A Jewish man was traveling on a trip from Jerusalem to Jericho, and he was attacked by bandits. They stripped him of his clothes, beat him up, and left him half dead beside the road.

By chance a priest came along. But when he saw the man lying there, he crossed to the other side of the road and passed him by.

A Temple assistant walked over and looked at him lying there, but he also passed by on the other side.

Then a despised Samaritan came along, and when he saw the man, he felt compassion for him. Going over to him, the Samaritan soothed his wounds with olive oil and wine and bandaged them.

Then he put the man on his own donkey and took him to an inn, where he took care of him. The next day he handed the innkeeper two silver coins, telling him, 'Take care of this man. If his bill runs higher than this, I'll pay you the next time I'm here.'

Now which of these three would you say was a neighbor to the man who was attacked by bandits?" Jesus asked.

The man replied, "The one who showed him mercy."

Then Jesus said, "Yes, now go and do the same."

In answer to your question, and with our Lord's words as our guide, I now have two questions for you.

"What does it say? How do you read it?"

Clearly, the lesson of *The Good Samaritan* story is that love encompasses the giving of ourselves– of our time, our attention, and even our financial resources– to help those in need. I believe it is impossible to read these words and get any other point of view.

Further, it is evident that this brand of love, filled with compassion, kindness and service, is quite important to the Lord.

After all, this was a discussion that began with a lawyer's inquiry into the requirements for his own salvation.

As we spoke of in a previous chapter, the answer that he receives is in the form of a descriptive tale that defines the meaning of such a love in very visual and easy-to-understand terms. Next, all ambiguity is removed over *whom* is to be covered by that love. And finally, the expectation is laid out, as Jesus gives this direction and command:

"...now go and do the same."

So, let's take a deep breath and acknowledge one fact.

This is often a bitter pill to swallow for some believers, because it can be a real struggle to get involved in any aspect of another's personal life– not to mention their health, and certainly not something as confrontational and potentially explosive as addiction.

This is especially true in the life of a casual acquaintance or stranger. Or worse: someone I dislike– even my enemy!

Yet, pick up your favorite translation of the Scriptures, or Google the phrase, *Bible Love*, and you'll find out that it's a pretty popular topic. In fact, with over 370,000,000 returned search results, you may find that you'll be having a long night tonight as well!

So what about this kind of love, and what about addiction? What have you learned?

Knowing the difficulties that you can come to expect in recovery, and looking at the following Biblical view of love's attributes, here is a question for you:

How many of these qualities do you think you may need when locked in a relationship with a victim of addiction– when denial runs rampant, when deceit becomes overwhelming, when blame is unbearable?

Found in the New Testament book of *First Corinthians*, here is one definition of the unconditional love that we are to possess– the same type of complete, forgiving, unconditional love and mercy that we daily receive from God as his children.

Go ahead and put a check mark next to each statement that you feel will be an asset to you in your current relationships and circumstances, and do a quick mental evaluation of those you feel are strengths or weaknesses for you:

> *"Love is patient and kind.*
> *Love is not jealous or boastful or proud or rude.*
> *It does not demand its own way.*
> *It is not irritable, and it keeps no record of being wronged.*
> *It does not rejoice about injustice,*
> *But rejoices whenever the truth wins out.*
> *Love never gives up,*
> *Never loses faith,*
> *Is always hopeful,*
> *And endures through every circumstance."*

Yes, Love endures... even through addiction.

YOUR OWN BEFORE AND AFTER

So how do you reach out?

How do you start that conversation?

You have just spent years going through the addiction grinder. Maybe first with a friend, and more recently with a family member, coworker, or fellow congregant.

You watched and prayed as your mom had surgery for heart disease, you hoped and prayed as your brother's attitude turned mean and his marriage failed. And you cried as you prayed for your son or daughter, who were out doing– well, who knows what, with who knows whom.

And now you've spent a few hours learning that you can make a difference; that you *are* the difference.

That you can use *The Samaritan Solution.*

Yes, you have begun to understand that the illnesses and diseases, the unkind attitudes, and the risky or destructive behaviors are likely mere symptoms of an underlying– and ultimately deadly– addictive condition, and what's more, you're starting to see it everywhere.

Yes, everywhere.

The teachers at your children's school and the neighbor across the street, your boss and your elected leaders, the strangers at the mall and the loved ones around the dinner table.

You now have taken notice of the heart disease and cancer, the high blood pressure and diabetes, the constant colds, coughing and doctor visits of people you know and love.

You've witnessed significant stress and pressure develop and affect them from seemingly minor issues. You've also seen the financial, emotional, and behavioral changes in their lives.

And you want it to stop– you're wondering what to do.

How do you let them know there's a solution?

How do you broach the subject?

How do you share your experience, strength, and hope?

All that you've gone through– all that you've learned?

Well, if your greatest weapons in the fight against addiction are your unconditional love and willingness to take correct action, your most effective tool for reaching others is your story.

Yes, your story.

Your own personal testimony– a short little before and after– is the key that can easily unlock a conversation without any threat of confrontation, and start another family on the road to healing and recovery.

Your story makes you relatable to others– approachable– and provides common ground on which to begin laying a foundation for recovery. As we have seen, all of the ailments and challenges that we face are fairly common experiences to hundreds of thousands– even millions– of other individuals and families, as well.

If we are listening, if we are aware, the conversations and the people crying out for help are all around. The question is whether or not we are willing to share of ourselves.

I remember this like it was yesterday: a simple shopping trip to the mall on one Black Friday– you know, the traditional retail frenzy that kicks off the Christmas season each year.

While standing in line at a grocery store, I offered a cordial greeting to a fellow shopper, "So, did you have a nice Thanksgiving?" Suddenly, this opened up a multiparty discussion among strangers about how stressful "this time of year" can be.

It was amazing.

Emotions spilled over the edge, producing excruciating details of broken families and broken relationships and broken hearts. How much pain and trepidation must have been boiling just under the surface for all of that to come out?

"I just *hate* this time of year," muttered one. "I know it's wrong, but that's how I feel."

Said another, "I'm just looking forward to getting through the next five weeks."

"Yes!" exclaimed the clerk at the checkout.

"Here's to the new year!"

The question, of course, is that if nothing really changes, what is going to be so different about next year?

After all, one thing is absolutely without debate: if their seasonal stress and depression have anything to do with addiction, left untreated, next year is going to be worse.

Possibly, *much* worse.

When I hear these things, I wonder whether this time, they might actually be interested to look under the tension that seems to routinely envelop them at various times of the year to find out what may be *causing* the trouble, the pain, and the uneasiness they feel?

Do they even want to know how to address what may be at the root of their unhappiness and despair?

More to the point, are they willing to be really honest about *why* their relationships are so strained, and to look at the role *they* may have played in creating the current turmoil? Further, what about *their own* ability to hurt others right now– to say and do the wrong things?

By now, you're asking the same questions too. After a while, all the symptoms take on a very similar look.

Regardless of what time of year you are reading this, here is what you need to know: as you speak with people and as these issues come up, not only are they indicators of an underlying addiction, but– thankfully– they are likely issues that you or someone close to you is also concerned with at this very moment.

You ask, "What is there to be thankful for in that?"

Well, it puts us all on the same page– in a place where we can talk about a subject that could bring healing to a family you know.

The top challenges that tens of millions of Americans are worried about at any given time are:

1) Health issues with themselves or a loved one,
2) Broken or strained relationships, and
3) Runaway debt or financial stress.

Sound familiar?

It is interesting to note that, regardless of demographics or geographical location, the same desires and concerns tend to wind through our culture. And they all have two things in common:

First, addiction is likely present in all of them.

And second, without exception, they have all been going on for a very long time. That's right– the same concerns that are on everyone's mind right now were the same that were on everyone's mind a year ago– and likely the year before that as well!

The progressive nature of addiction guarantees it.

And, since it has proven to be stronger than the human will, the addict cannot simply decide to quit.

Without help, without getting to the cause, we've already seen that the average resolution made going into the new year will last less than three weeks, and the average resolution made at any other time of the year will not even last that long. After a few short days of struggle with whatever withdrawal symptoms come along, over 93% of Americans will cave.

They will go back to using the substance or engaging in the behavior, while they begin to hope for more willpower in the future.

Yes, in each case, they will tell themselves that they are simply regrouping to fight another day. However, the truth is that they are literally killing themselves, *one day at a time.*

Suddenly, enter your story.

"I know exactly how you feel. I went through the very same thing, and here's what I did." The energy that is contained in those simple words breathes hope and light and life into the world of someone who, only moments before, was full of hopelessness and darkness and desperation.

"Oh my goodness! If you did it, then maybe I can do it too!"
The effects are unmistakable, and powerful.
Yes, this happened to me too!
Yes, our family was just like yours!
Yes, we were crumbling also!
Yes, we did something about it... and you can, too!
Powerful, indeed!

Over the years, I have personally witnessed the life-giving and history-altering power of personal stories– my own, and others.

Certainly, this is true with families who are in the middle of the storm and who are unaware that there are solutions even available to them.

But they are also just as engaging and meaningful to individuals and families who have been involved in the recovery process for quite some time.

A few years ago, I met several women who were part of a Twelve Step group for those suffering with food addiction. And as I think of our interaction now, I'm sure they remember meeting me as well!

As we spoke, I confided to this group that, indeed, like them, I was also a food addict.

The room exploded and I'm sure their response could have been heard in the building next door!

"Hahahahahahaha!! You? A food addict?? You certainly don't look like a food addict!"

Hmm...

Now, this is critical:

I asked, with all due respect, what a food addict is supposed to look like. More to the point, what is a food addict *in recovery* supposed to look like.

You see, each of these women, again with all due respect, *did* look like they had an addiction to food.

Each was at least seventy or eighty pounds overweight.

Each was ill with the standard complications and diseases.

Each was slowly dying.

And that is what is so sad, because it didn't need to happen.

No, I suppose I don't look like a food addict.

Having lost 183 pounds on the program and keeping it off will do that for you.

Now, it's amazing, but when you share that story– the story of complete recovery– a funny thing happens: people see hope, and their eyes light up, often for the very first time.

"Yes," they whisper to themselves, "it *is* possible..."

So what is the most important component of your story?

Well, in my opinion, and as highlighted by the previous example, there *is no* story without your own recovery first. You see, your experience, strength and hope is rooted in:

1) Life circumstances that were highly destructive,
2) A solution that was implemented, and
3) Results that lead to healing and restoration.

All three are necessary. If we have only point number one, our conversation will be built on a foundation of gossip, commiseration, or sympathy. Yes, we're in the same boat– and we're all going down with the ship!

Go back to the parable. What story could have been told by the first two who passed by?

"Oh, it was terrible. As I rounded the bend, there he was: beaten, bloody, bruised. I don't even think he was really alive anymore. It was so sad... but there was nothing that I could do."

That's it. Not much of a story, is it?

And what if we had only the first two points– a problem and a solution, but no results? That might sound like this:

"Yes, I know exactly how you feel. We had the identical situation with a cousin, and here's what we did."

Great, and how'd that work out for you?

"Uh, well... uh, yeah, well... uhm... he died."

What?!

Where is the strength, the encouragement, the hope in *that?*

Answer: there is none.

Among other things, your triumph over addiction exists to help others, and it comes alive in your own personal story of recovery. Not surprisingly, that requires a situation in which you and your family actually recovered!

Now, you can boldly proclaim, "Yes, I understand where you are– more importantly, let me share with you where you could be!"

So, my Samaritan friend, this is why your leadership is so important. You must stand firm to do whatever it takes to see the process through to a successful recovery.

You must develop your own story to share your experience, strength and hope. And you must be willing to do it right now for the one whom you love. Because, as a believer, the expectation is that you be willing to provide it for anyone else who may need it as you travel your own road to Jericho.

We wish you, your family, and your loved ones complete recovery. We pray for your restoration. And we believe that the plan you desire, and the peace that you seek, is now within your grasp– for you have received the ultimate solution, *The Samaritan Solution.*

Epilogue

*   *   *

In The Name Of Love

At one time or another, every single person who has ever experienced any form of addiction in their life or relationships has found themselves sitting right smack-dab in the exact same chair that you find yourself in now.

The questions and concerns are identical, as is your desire to create a new and different set of circumstances in your present life or the life of someone you care about deeply.

Like you, we have all spent much time alternately fighting or dreaming, arguing or grieving, overwhelmed or wishing.

And like you, we have never given up hoping, trying, working, learning, loving, searching, and praying.

There are so many thoughts that may be racing through your mind right now– so many unknowns for tomorrow.

Will there be difficult days ahead?
Count on it.
Can waking up ever feel good again?
Absolutely.
Is it possible for real love to return to your home and family?
Without a doubt– it already has.

This may be difficult to see and feel right now– you may be hurting so intensely. However, I pray that you will understand the next statement clearly:

You *hurt* so much... because you *love* so much.

Like the Good Samaritan, it is *your love* that decided to stop while others passed by– your love that recognized the danger signs and the severity of the situation.

It is your love that put you on a search for answers and options, to increase your knowledge and ability to help others who may be totally unaware of the root cause of their difficulty.

It is your love that will give you a heart of compassion and a willingness to act without regard to selfish concerns– to do what you can do personally, and then enlist the assistance of others.

It is your love that will allow you to guide and to lead and to make right choices and difficult decisions during extreme moments– decisions that could ultimately break the chains of addiction for someone in your family, your neighborhood, your workplace or your house of worship.

And it is your love which placed *The Samaritan Solution* into your hands, and kept you up all night reading right on through to the final pages of this epilogue!

A few minutes ago, I said that love had already returned to your home and family.

You are that love.

Yes, you are the love in your house.

You are the love in your relationships.

You are the love in the life of someone who, right now, feels totally and absolutely and genuinely *unlovable*.

And you are not alone– as a believer, you are *never* alone.

God is love.

He has promised never to leave you.

God loves you, and He loves your family, your friends, and those whom you are most concerned about at this very minute.

That is the message of Jesus.

We love *God* because He first loved us.

And we love *others...* because He first loved us.

This is the world's most powerful love letter– a letter which has transcended time just so that you could receive its beautiful message in your life today– right in the middle of your storm.

The Samaritan Solution is simple. Love God and love your neighbor– even in a culture of addiction.

Endnotes

Thanks to Bible History Online:
http://www.bible-history.com/geography/ancient-israel/jericho.html
for background context and translation of the name, Jericho,
The City of Palm Trees and Place of Fragrance.

* * *

Additional details regarding Positron Emission Tomography (PET) and Magnetic
Resonance Imaging (MRI) as used in addiction medicine can be found at:
The University of Utah, Genetic Science Learning Center,
Learn More About Brain Imaging Technologies,
http://learn.genetics.utah.edu/content/addiction/drugs/brainimage.html

The American Society of Addiction Medicine has published the following
definition of addiction:
http://www.asam.org/for-the-public/definition-of-addiction

* * *

Throughout the book, we have used statistics indicating the use of addictive
substances, the exercise of addictive behaviors, as well as the relative impacts to
our society, our citizens, our health care system, and our economy. These have
been compiled from a number of sources, most notably:

The Centers For Disease Control and Prevention, http://www.cdc.gov
the National Institute on Alcohol Abuse and Alcoholism, http://www.niaaa.nih.gov
and the National Institutes of Health, an agency of the Department of Health and
Human Services, http://health.nih.gov

We found some variance in these reports and estimates due to the data collection
methods used by the various organizations and governmental bodies involved. In
each case where this was apparent, we made the effort to use the most
conservative statistics possible.

* * *

You may find statistics regarding pornography from the
Center for Christian Broadcasting at:
http://christianbroadcasting.org/index.php?
option=com_content&view=article&id=55:waging-war-sexual-addiction

And TechMission Inc's program, Safe Families at:
http://www.safefamilies.org/sfStats.php

* * *

Further, there are terrific and enlightening insights on excess weight and obesity
from the National Center for Health Statistics at:
http://nchspressroom.wordpress.com/2009/01/14/new-health-e-stat-integrates-
obesity-and-overweight-prevalence-data/

Also from Stanford University Hospitals and Clinics at:
http://stanfordhospital.org/clinicsmedServices/COE/surgicalServices/generalSurge
ry/bariatricsurgery/obesity/effects.html

And from this report from Fox News,
http://www.foxnews.com/story/0,2933,478964,00.html

* * *

Data on smoking-related usage and effects can be found at:
http://www.cdc.gov/tobacco/data_statistics/fact_sheets/health_effects/effects_cig_
smoking/

The history of polio– its rise, fall and eradication, as well as the founding of the
March of Dimes organization– can be found at:
http://www.npr.org/templates/story/story.php?storyId=4585992 and
http://www.marchofdimes.com/mission/history.html

* * *

We used US population estimates found from:
http://www.infoplease.com/ipa/A0004986.html

And prescription data found at:
http://www.pharmacist.com/am/customsource/mtm/Booklet/APhA-NASPA - Key to Improving Medication Use WI Booklet 11x17.pdf for 2007 Wisconsin prescriptions

http://www.pharmacist.com/am/customsource/mtm/single_pages/APhA-NASPA - Key to Improving Medication Use Missouri 8.5x11.pdf for 2007 Missouri prescriptions

http://www.pharmacist.com/am/customsource/mtm/Booklet/APhA-NASPA - Key to Improving Medication Use IL Booklet 11x17.pdf for 2007 Illinois prescriptions

* * *

There are revealing trends in medical prescriptions here:
http://www.cdc.gov/nchs/data/databriefs/db42.pdf
as well as here: http://www.cdc.gov/nchs/fastats/drugs.htm
and from the Kaiser Family Foundation:
http://www.kff.org/rxdrugs/upload/3057_07.pdf

* * *

Caveat Emptor is defined by Cornell University Law School here:
http://www.law.cornell.edu/wex/Caveat_emptor

* * *

One of the first to chronicle the circumstances surrounding the Kitty Genovese murder was author and eventual New York Times editor Abe Rosenthal: A.M. Rosenthal, *Thirty-Eight Witnesses* (1964).

A collection of other articles regarding this case can be found at the New York Times' website at:
http://www.nytimes.com/keyword/kitty-genovese

Further thanks to Malcolm Gladwell, New York Times bestselling author and speaker, for key insights which can be found here:
Malcolm Gladwell, *The Tipping Point: How Little Things Can Make A Big Difference* (2000), pp. 27-28

The term "pluralistic ignorance" was coined by Daniel Katz and Floyd H. Allport in: *Students' Attitudes: A Report of the Syracuse University Reaction Study* (1931).

* * *

The BBC covered both the Prince Charles/Lady Diana wedding and the Princess Diana funeral on the following websites:
http://news.bbc.co.uk/onthisday/hi/dates/stories/july/29/newsid_2494000/2494949.stm

http://news.bbc.co.uk/onthisday/hi/dates/stories/september/6/newsid_2502000/2502307.stm

* * *

The principles and insights introduced in an excellent article by Sid Goodman are evident in our book and are helpful to any serious discussion regarding treatment and recovery from addiction.

Read more here:

Sid Goodman, MA, LMHC, Executive Director/Clinical Director, Caron Renaissance, *Psychodynamic Approach to Addiction Treatment*:
http://www.caronrenaissance.org/media_center/files/PsychodynamicApproachtoAddictionTreatment.pdf

* * *

You will find that the signs of addiction are available through many and various sources, including books, 12 Step programs, and websites. With millions of words written on this topic, and with symptoms for all addictions running a similar course, it is possible for phrases or concepts to overlap.

The signs of addiction suggested in this book, however, are gathered from the experience of 40+ years in private practice, without regard or reference to other materials, and any similarity to other works is purely coincidental.

*   *   *

Workbook
And
Action Guide

Breaking it down into its three most fundamental properties, success in using *The Samaritan Solution* to combat addiction entails these factors:

1) A willingness to be involved in helping our neighbor,

2) The ability to accurately identify the likely cause, and

3) The knowledge to avoid critical mistakes while getting proper help and assistance for your loved one.

As you work through the following questions and chapter reviews, you will receive deeper insight and understanding into the thoughts and emotions that are so common in the process of addiction recovery.

In addition to identifying and clarifying areas of strength and weakness in your own approach, you will also have the opportunity to contrast your views and beliefs with others in your circle of friends and family whose input and involvement may be critically important to the recovery effort.

For this purpose, it is recommended that each of your friends or family members who are involved in the process read *The Samaritan Solution*, and then answer the following questions.

This Workbook And Action Guide is also available as an

attractively bound 8"x10" publication that gives you plenty of room to write as you study and reflect on over 300 in-depth questions (order separately for just $4.95 through Amazon.com).

We believe you will find this guide helpful as a family or small group discussion resource, and also as an introspective, personal journal that summarizes your own knowledge and comprehension of this complex and demanding subject.

Finally, as a tool to identify and pinpoint mistakes that may have been made in the past, many people find it useful to view each question in two separate contexts: first, in terms of their historical beliefs on a given question, and secondly, contrasting that answer with their present understanding of the same topic today.

For example, prior to reading *The Samaritan Solution*, one may have thought nothing of their friend's eating habits and subsequent weight gain that took place after their friend stopped smoking.

"Oh, it happens all the time," they once thought. "Everyone knows that people often gain weight after they quit smoking!"

Yes, that's true. But now, you know why.

Now, you know that beating the cigarettes did not beat the moving target called addiction.

And, more importantly, now you are in the position to be a hero, a Good Samaritan.

We wish you health, healing, and impact,
and we're thankful to have you on the team.
The Lord's Blessings to you and yours.

Questions Raised In The Introduction

- Up until this point, what has been your prevailing view of addiction? Have you thought of it mostly in terms of alcohol or drugs? Or have you considered it in terms of any substance, behavior, or activity that creates dependence and aberrant withdrawal symptoms? How has your view shaped your past actions or interest in becoming involved, positively or negatively?

- What is your understanding of the causes of addiction? Do you see it as the payment for bad choices and rebellious behavior? Or as a disease with physiological and chemical roots within the body's systems?

- Have you ever felt as if addiction couldn't happen to you and your family? Or not to those in your circle of friends, neighbors, and relatives? How about to those at your work or house of worship?

- Have you ever previously considered that many of the problems within our society, and within our churches, synagogues and families, may have had addiction as the root cause all along? How will this concept affect how you view what appear to be otherwise common illnesses in the future?

- In your own words, how does the parable of *The Good Samaritan* apply to your life in the present time? How have you played the part of the hero? Have you ever stood by, turned away, or passed by while a brother or sister struggled with physical, emotional, or spiritual illness? Have you ever been the victim? What do you believe Jesus would have us do regarding addiction?

- How long have there been health concerns with your friend or loved one? What has been done to help them to date? Are you hopeful? Hopeless?

Chapter 1 – Scenes On The Path To Prosperity

- What are the events that can happen between childhood and adulthood that have the potential to steal joy from our lives? Have you previously considered how these factors may be related to addiction? Do you see any of these concerns in your own life? In the lives of those you love?

- How do people use the pursuit of prosperity to hide what may in reality be troubling symptoms of addiction in their lives? Do we tend to gloss over the possibility of addiction when the victim is someone who is very close to us? How about if they are extremely prominent or financially successful?

- Have you ever felt alone in dealing with addiction of a loved one? Ever pondered the question, "Why me?" Is it, or has it been, your belief that addiction is common throughout society? What do the Scriptures say about those conditions from which we suffer?

- Can you think of any famous people– politicians, sports figures, or celebrities– who have been brought down by addictions to drugs or alcohol? How about food, gambling or sex? What about those who may have succumbed to addiction-related diseases like heart disease or cancer? Where were their handlers, and why might they have avoided help?

- With all the money spent in the various "wars" on drugs, alcohol abuse, smoking, and obesity– and with all the resources targeted to combat life threatening diseases– are the rates of these common ailments significantly dropping or are they on the rise? Why do you think that is so?

- Have the percentages increased or decreased for those involved in substance abuse, obesity, and pornography? How about the numbers of those taking prescription medications? Are you or anyone you know taking them?

- How can activities such as gambling, pornography, or shopping affect the chemical stimulation of the addict's brain? How do these changes lead to tolerance and the drive for increased use and abuse?

- Is there any way of predicting in advance who may or may not become a victim of addiction? How important– or non-important– are variables such as socioeconomic factors, family history, or early intervention?

Chapter 2 – Falling Amongst Thieves

- If you read the parable of *The Good Samaritan* to your child or grandchild, what are the chances they would understand the concept? If you changed the context– the victim is stranded in a snow storm or lost at sea without food, or yes, struggling with disease and addiction– do you believe your child would still get it? What can we learn from our children?

- If addiction is present in the life of a friend or family member, do you believe it is likely to resolve itself? Is it reasonable to expect that the addict's willpower can defeat it? Why or why not?

- How about your love and concern alone– can they defeat addiction? What is the worst-case scenario if your friend or loved one receives no help or treatment? What's the best case? Is the difference worth getting involved?

- In what terms do most Americans define the word success? How would most people say that addiction fits into that definition? If I told you that Jimmy was an addict, and then asked your perception of his level of success in life, what would you say? What if I told you he had heart disease, and then asked the same question? Is your answer different, and if so, why?

- What does the phrase, "We are as sick as our secrets," mean to you? What if we add the word "only," to make it, "We are *only* as sick as our secrets?" With whom can you speak about your addiction concerns? Are they able to guide and direct you with a step-by-step plan? Are you on that plan now, and if so, are you confident with the results?

- In your own words, define the disease of addiction. What is the natural progression that addiction follows? Where is your friend or loved one on this scale right now? Have they been there before?

- What percentage of our population under the age of twenty-five admits to using illegal drugs? How many young people do you know in that age range? How many are within your church, or your family? What are the chances that they've all beaten the odds? Could many of their parents be in denial?

- On average, how do addictions to alcohol and tobacco play out in the lives of their victims? How pervasive are addictions to gambling and pornography in our society today? How do those addictions affect the lives of their victims and victims' families?

- What substance is the greatest threat to the health of our nation? In terms of recovery, what separates food addiction from all other addictions? How do food addictions manifest themselves in the health of their victims?

- What ingredients in food cause the most trouble for food addicts? What organ of the body is most affected by the culprits?

- What chemical changes take place, and what cravings result?

- How do withdrawal symptoms from food differ from those of other addictions? How treatable is food addiction?

- Have you ever witnessed an individual who seemingly beat one substance or activity, only to fall into another?

- Have you known someone who quit drinking, but increased their smoking? Or stopped smoking, but gained thirty pounds? How does this pattern fit into our definition of addiction as a progressive series of behaviors?

- If your loved one dies from Addiction B, C, or D, does it matter that they beat Addiction A?

Chapter 3 – Menace To Society

- What are the differences between the way society perceives various addictions? How do we see the alcoholic who takes out a lamp post with their car versus the grandmother who provides sugar cookies to her little ones just a week after her own open heart surgery? What about grandma versus the sex addict who just trashed his marriage, or the smoker dying of emphysema?

- Do most addicts understand the the consequences of their actions? Do they want to cause pain, anger, and shame? Why don't they just quit? How is the body's immune system challenged by addiction? Who can really help them?

- Do you believe the politicians understand addiction? Why or why not?

- What effect will taxing a substance have on the rate of addiction to that substance? Has it worked with alcohol? Cigarettes? Will it work with soda and fast food? How confident are you in a government solution to stem the epidemics of heart disease, diabetes, cancer, high blood pressure and anxiety disorders?

- Does it matter who pays for a treatment if the diagnosis is missed in the first place? From all that you have seen, does it appear that a political solution will result in more accurate identification, better prevention, and higher quality care? Does throwing money at addiction's symptoms make the cause go away? How much money did the Kings of Pop and Rock and Roll throw at theirs?

- Do you believe the medical community understands addiction? Why or why not?

- What is the last major disease that was virtually wiped from the planet? How many years ago was that? Do you believe that cures for common illnesses are beyond the scope of today's medical technology?

- Outside of antibiotics, do pharmaceutical drugs typically treat the causes of disease, or the symptoms of disease? Are you clear about the distinction between the two?

- How frequently is addiction considered in diagnosing the cause of such diseases as heart disease, cancer, high blood pressure, obesity, anorexia, bulimia, stroke and diabetes? What are the most common treatments for those ailments?

- To what degree does the medical community suffer from the same diseases? Is it possible to prevent the onset or worsening of these ailments without drugs? How often is the prescription for health a non-pharmaceutical solution? Why do you believe that is so? What is the average response to a prescription of a pharmaceutical drug? Have you ever refused to take it?

- How much of a burden is placed on our economy by managing a lifetime of illness, as opposed to eradicating the illness? How much emphasis is placed on continually improving the health of our people versus the need for providing more managed care of an increasingly unhealthy nation?

- Who are the financial losers in a game where the treatment of a healthy society is no longer necessary because of the elimination of disease? Between curing illness and managing illness, what course of action has the greatest incentive for the medical community?

- Do you believe the pharmaceutical industry understands addiction? Why or why not?

- Do pharmaceutical solutions typically cure the ailment or just make it manageable? If you tried to create a list of all the prescription medications that contain no side effects, how long would it be? How about those with dangerous complications and side effects?

- What organs of the body are most stressed by pharmaceutical drugs of any kind? How often is the solution for the side effect of a prescription drug, yet another prescription drug?

- What has been the pharmaceutical industry's track record with respect to aiding recovery from addiction? Has addiction-related disease declined or increased over the past generation? What is Big Pharma's solution to heart disease, high blood pressure and diabetes? What are some of the factors that all of these diseases have in common?

- With the equivalent of eleven prescriptions written for every man, woman, and child in the country, why do you believe there is so little outcry? Are you or any family members on any prescriptions right now? If there was another solution, would you want to know about it?

- Do you believe the insurance companies understand addiction? Why or why not?

- What is the likely response of underwriters if they find out about a potential addiction circumstance with one of their policy holders? Do their actions indicate a belief in the ability of the addict to recover?

- What programs could be funded through insurance to encourage preventative behavior? What is the rationale behind denying the most effective treatments for alcoholism, substance abuse and food addiction– while agreeing to pay for long-term care when those addictions progress into heart disease, cancer, high blood pressure, stroke and diabetes? How will the proposed reforms to insurance coverage help find solutions for addiction recovery? Do you have confidence in an insurance-based solution for addiction?

- Do you believe the fitness industry understands addiction? Why or why not?

- If excess weight is at the heart of so many diseases, why are the majority of club members unable to maintain a healthy weight in spite of working out like mad at their club? What is the Achilles Heel of working out with strenuous exercise? How can individuals mask their hidden addictions by exercising excessively?

- Do you believe our justice system understands addiction? Why or why not?

- How does the threat of medical malpractice suits lead to the treatment of symptoms, as opposed to an underlying addiction?

- Knowing that addiction often leads to criminal behavior, how is an addict helped by receiving a slap-on-the-wrist sentence? What is the likely outcome? On the other hand, what are the chances of rehabilitation in a correctional system that is replete with other addicts? Once in the system, what is the recidivism rate? Does the justice system seem to offer real solutions?

- Do you believe our media understands addiction? Why or why not?

- What one industry could most effectively get the word out about recovery? With a 96% recovery rate possible, what do you believe encourages the media to focus on the train-wrecks? How often do you hear the good news of recovery on major media? How often do you hear good news at all? What is the revenue model that finances the media's news broadcasts and operations?

- How much money flows in through advertising from politicians, the medical community, drug and insurance companies, fitness centers, and the lawyers? How powerful are their lobbies? How interested do you believe they are in finding a solution to addiction? How interested do you believe any of them is in learning that the cause of many of their own problems is addiction?

- Do you believe the food industry understands addiction? Why or why not?

- What addiction is at the heart of the health crisis in America? How has our food industry, with packaging and additives and preservatives, changed over the last forty years? How have those changes correlated with obesity rates and skyrocketing instances of weight-related maladies like heart disease, high blood pressure, cancer, stroke and diabetes? What is the number one factor in the the explosion of juvenile diabetes?

- What three ingredients are most harmful to Americans in general, and food addicts in particular? How many ways has the food industry found to conceal sugar and its equivalents in our diets? Why do you believe some people in our society demand more and more products of convenience, even as those products are conveniently killing them?

Chapter 4 – My Brother's Keeper

- What thoughts and memories did you have as you read the story about Kitty Genovese? What application does that story have for your life? To addiction? Did you make any decisions? How does that story correlate to the Lord's parable of *The Good Samaritan*?

- Is there someone in your life who is crying out for help? Are the symptoms of the attack going unnoticed? Is addiction a possible cause? Can someone else be trusted to intervene, or is it up to you?

- Have you ever reached out in the past to help, only to feel as though the situation got worse? If so, what happened? Do you know of any situations where family or friends engaged in denial over their loved one's addiction? Or felt shame, guilt, or embarrassment?

- How did those emotions help or hinder the recovery process? Have you ever heard someone advocate the concept of hitting bottom? Have you ever used that phrase yourself? Have you witnessed the bottom personally?

- How does enabling hurt the recovery effort? Have you or other friends or family members ever covered for the conduct or behavior of a loved one who's addicted? If so, what forms has that taken? What were the results?

- Have you ever used anger or confrontation, or maybe ostracized your friend or loved one? What were those results? What other solutions have you tried in the past? Are you willing to try again?

Chapter 5 – Everyday Heroes

- What is the one quality that is common to heroes of any kind? Do you possess that quality? What price are you willing to pay to see through the recovery of your friend or loved one? What example can we take from the parable of *The Good Samaritan*? And what aspect of the Samaritan's behavior led to him receiving the adjective of being "good?"

- How do you identify with the actions of the Samaritan? What decisions have you made? Why do you believe some otherwise caring individuals are willing to "pass by" to avoid involvement in recovery? What excuses do they use?

- What does Scripture say in response to the question of being our brother's keeper? What relevance does it have in our lives today?

- What message is given specifically to believers regarding the Lord's expectations for our relationship to our fellow man or woman? Do you believe it has special meaning for those in our nation's churches and synagogues?

- Why do you believe so many people in our houses of worship have such an aversion to the topic of addiction? According to every survey, how do those "in the faith" line up with those "outside the faith" in terms of addiction and its complications?

- What is the pervasive view of addiction within the community of believers? What do you believe Jesus would do with any of the addicts in your life? What would He ask of you? What is He asking of you?

Chapter 6 – Caution: Danger Ahead

- Why do so many miss the early warning signs of addiction? What do we tell ourselves at first sight?

- On the next few pages we will look at the following warning signs of addiction:
  1) Financial
  2) Physical
  3) Metal and Emotional
  4) Spiritual

5)   Social
6)   Relational
7)   Behavioral

- Have you seen any of the following issues in yourself or a loved one? If so, note the name(s) of any individual(s) who bring these concerns to mind. To help organize your thoughts, break it down by extended family, fellow members at your house of worship and friends or coworkers.

Financial Signs

- The most common financial signs of addiction are job loss, continuing unemployment, money that disappears, bankruptcy or a sudden onset of late payments or creditor calls. Do you know anyone in any of those boats? List any or all who come to mind as you consider the symptoms.

Physical Signs

- The most common physical signs of addiction are the known use of addictive substances such as alcohol, drugs, tobacco, and unhealthy foods, or the engagement in addictive activities or behaviors such as gambling, pornography, and compulsive shopping. Other physical symptoms include tiredness, frequent aches, pains and irritability, excessive or insufficient weight, frequent illness, and serious ailments such as heart disease, high blood pressure, cancer or diabetes, as well as a lack of sexual interest or impotence. List any or all who come to mind as you consider those symptoms.

Mental and Emotional Signs

• The most common mental and emotional signs of addiction are depression, insomnia, anxiety and panic attacks, as well as bouts of confusion, anger, sadness and thoughts of suicide, or periods of blackouts, paranoia and forgetfulness. List any or all who come to mind as you consider the symptoms.

Spiritual Signs

• The most common spiritual signs of addiction are a sense of hopelessness and apathy, feelings of desperation regarding the future, and thoughts of death and suicide. Additionally, the neglect of core values, low self-image and self-worth, and feelings of guilt, shame, fear, and abandonment are cause for concern. If anyone came to mind as you considered those symptoms, please put down this book and call me now, 24/7, or dial 911.

Social Signs

• The most common social signs of addiction are friendships and associations with others who are suspected or known users of addictive substances such as alcohol, drugs, tobacco, and unhealthy foods, or the engagement in addictive activities or behaviors such as gambling, pornography, and compulsive shopping. Also, associations which are based on risky behaviors, or with individuals who have a history of frequent trouble or run-ins with the law. List any or all who come to mind as you consider the symptoms.

Relational Signs

- The most common relational signs of addiction are a gradual withdrawal from friends and family, lack of opinions on important issues, reserved temperament and unwillingness to share life, or a discontinued involvement in events, hobbies, and once-common interests. List any or all who come to mind as you consider the symptoms.

Behavioral Signs

- The most common behavioral signs of addiction are blame, deceit, denial, and anger, especially when confronted with the concerns of you or other friends and family. List any or all who come to mind as you consider the symptoms.

- It is likely there are now several names on at least a few of these lists. In fact, most people have fifteen or more names in mind or on paper by this point. Whatever your number, take heart– it just means you have true Samaritan potential!

Chapter 7 – Compassion And Action

- What do you think we should do with the list you just generated in the last section? Keep the names handy, fix them firmly in your mind, and then answer these questions: what would the hero of our story do now? Yes, in fact, what would Jesus do? What will you do?

- As defined in this chapter, what is the difference between sympathy and compassion, and which did the Samaritan possess? How do the emotions of pity and sorrow fit into the equation, if at all? What does compassion require of us?

- At this point, why do so many friends and family want to turn the options and decision-making process over to the addict– in effect, to someone who is slowly and methodically killing themselves, and unable to think clearly?

- Would they ask the victim what to do if that person were having a heart attack instead? Or would they call 911 and yell for help? What is the difference?

- If addiction is at the root of the problem, what can you expect to happen next? Based on the addict's past performance, do you trust them to make the decisions that are in their best interests? In the family's best interest? Right now, with this book in your hands, who is the most qualified member of your circle of family and friends to do the right thing?

- What help can you expect as you move this process forward? Who will be team players? Which members of the inner circle are most likely to cave? To enable? To look for shortcuts? You will need a plan for when that happens. Do you have one? Does everyone know his or her part?

- Have you searched for easy solutions? What have you found? Online? In book stores? On television or radio or direct mail ads? Why are families who are dealing with addiction such easy targets for marketers of pure fluff? Have you fallen for any claims? What were they? Do you have a solution you can implement today?   Who will lead and orchestrate the process?

- What are the three components to a successful recovery package?   When implemented separately, what are the standard results that one can expect? Why is rehab such an important component? What do the family and the addict derive from Twelve Step fellowships? Why is counseling so powerful, and what roles does it fulfill? What results can be expected by putting the whole approach together?

Chapter 8 – Great Expectations

- Imagine your loved one is entering rehab this week. What are your thoughts and emotions? What do you want to tell them?

- Some cases require great involvement on the part of the family, others not so much. What commitments are you willing to make to provide the best environment for recovery? What is most challenging for you to consider? Financial commitments? Time commitments? Who else is right now committed to travel this road with you? What is their experience? What is their track record under fire?

- Whom do you know who has achieved and maintained long-term sobriety of at least ten years? Are they part of your inner circle?

- Whom do you know who has ridden the roller coaster of abstinence and relapse over and over? What do you believe are the most critical factors influencing long-term success or failure? Presently, what is the status of those factors in your loved one's case?

- Fix in your mind an individual whom you know to possess any of the symptoms of addiction described earlier, and then answer this question: are they living in an environment where others are also exhibiting symptoms of addiction? For example, Bobby is smoking marijuana, and this has everyone concerned. However, no one seems to consider addiction in the case of his father, who smokes cigarettes, his mother, who has diabetes and is overweight, or his friends, who all seem to drink too much.

- What are examples of addictions to substances which are perfectly legal and even promoted in America?

- Why are these addictions often so much more difficult to diagnose and treat than, say, an addiction to illicit drugs such as cocaine or methamphetamine? What are some things that can be done to create more awareness to these other addictions? What are you willing to do?

- What are some examples of ordinary situations or events that contain perilous potential for an individual addicted to alcohol, drugs, gambling, sex, or food?

- Why are holidays frequently so damaging to one's ability to remain abstinent? What are some of the most common ways that simple family functions create an atmosphere for relapse? What is one concrete change you could champion immediately to ensure that this danger is reduced in your home, place of work, or house of worship? How do proper rest and nutrition fit into the recovery equation?

- On a scale of 1-10, how important are issues of health and proper nutrition to you? How about to the others in your household and in the addict's sphere of influence?

- Knowing that improper nutrition and addictive foods can trigger relapses for other addictions, are you committed to eliminating these substances from your home? Do you have a plan? Are you willing to read more about this connection?

Chapter 9 – Do The Same

- Theoretically, what would be the most efficient way to reach the world with the good news of recovery? How likely is that scenario, and are you willing to be a Samaritan anyway? Are you willing to e-mail some links to some online resources? How about purchasing a few extra copies of a book– this book, *The Samaritan Solution*– and giving them out to a family member or other friends in need?

- Considering the concept of grace, how has God's favor manifested itself in your life, or in the lives of those you love? Can you perceive His grace as being present, even in light of your loved one's addiction?

- What are three examples from the past year in which His love and protection were evident? What actions does the Scriptural model mandate for those of us who would be His followers?

- As believers, is there a higher calling than just living a life of success? If so, what is the path to such significance? Citing your own experience, what is the Eleventh Commandment, and what connection does it have in relationship to those suffering from addiction?

- What does the term, "unconditional love," mean to you? How have you applied it successfully in the past? What is one example in which you have struggled with it recently? How can your story and your experience provide strength and hope to others? Can you engage a total stranger by concisely stating your own personal before-and-after in thirty seconds or less?

Developing Your Story

If you struggle with the idea of how to engage others with your personal story in thirty seconds or less, don't worry– most do. We'll construct that story together in just a minute. The idea is simply this:

If we have been helped ourselves,
If we have had a spiritual awakening,
If we have been shown grace,
If we have experienced recovery,

And if the command is to go and do the same...

Then, we must be able to provide that testimony in an easy and non-threatening way. We must be able to share our experience, strength and hope in a focused, simple and direct format.

Here's the powerful message that you are communicating: Yes, I know exactly how you feel– I was there too. May I tell you what happened?

Those words are like pure gold to an individual or family that is struggling in the chaos of addiction!

"Yes, *please* tell me! Tell me there is hope, and a future! Tell me that all is not lost, that we haven't tried everything yet! Yes, tell me how you survived– where you were, and where you are now! And please, tell me that it can work for us also!"

When telling your story, you don't need to write a book– though I must admit this has been fun! I am simply suggesting that you confidently engage your brother or sister– thirty seconds, max– and open a door for them to get more information and help.

So here is what you do:
Think of your path through addiction and recovery. Think of the lowest spot, and write down those thoughts and feelings. Next, make a list of what changes have occurred– what you did, and what has happened as a result.
Put it in terms of the emotions that you were feeling or continue to feel. Go ahead...

Need help getting started?

Here are examples of how a "before" statement might sound:

"I was hopeless, angry, tired and bitter."
"I was worried day and night."
"I couldn't sleep."
"My nerves were shot."
"We were fighting all the time."
"Our lives were filled with shame and embarrassment."
"We were afraid to answer the phone or the door. "
"I just wanted it to end... I wanted it all to end."

Imagine that.

You have already felt and experienced all of the same types of pain and the same kinds of emotions that the person next to you is feeling right now.

And if you can share that– with love, and without judgment– there will likely be connection. And a conversation of hope evolves.

You can put it all together.
Tell them what you did.
Yes, please share with them the rest of the story...

"We tried everything we knew, but nothing worked. Then we read this book– we got some real help– and, most importantly, we got our mom back!"

Finally, hone your story. Keep a journal, and as you read and learn, as you attend meetings and meet others who have traveled the same roads, make notes as you hear their stories. As you sense their emotions, you'll find that you have experienced many of them yourself.

These are the stories that impact, the stories that move, the stories that inspire action and the stories that begin to heal.

Simple stories. Life-saving stories.

In three easy pieces:

"We were where you are now."
"We took action."
"We have life again– and so can you."

Write your story now below:

"I know exactly how you feel..." (tell your experience) _____

_____

_____

_____

_____

"May I share with you what we did?" (tell your solution) _____

_____

_____

_____

_____

"Since then..." (tell your results) _____

_____

_____

_____

_____

Epilogue – In The Name Of Love

- Express your understanding of the true nature and depth of God's love toward His creation. What does He expect from us in return? What are some of the ways that we can make this tangible in our everyday lives? How does it relate to the issues of strife, illness and addiction in our homes and places of work and worship?

- What message does our willingness to love others unconditionally send to the world at large? How about our unwillingness to love?

Ready To Make An Impact?

Want to share the hope of recovery and restoration with those struggling with addiction? Here are a dozen ways that you can help to make a difference today!

1) Buy *The Samaritan Solution* book and begin applying the principles and healing your relationships today.

2) Buy additional stacks of the paperback books to give as gifts to friends and family or share with health professionals, clergy, or ministry staff. Volume discounts are available– contact us for details.

3) Shine the light by telling your coworkers, neighbors and relatives about http://www.samaritansolution.com/ and encourage them to get a copy for themselves.

4) Email the link http://www.samaritansolution.com/ to friends in high places, along with local news outlets, business leaders and politicians.

5) Become a Fan of *The Samaritan Solution* on Facebook at http://www.facebook.com/TheSamaritanSolution.

6) Promote *The Samaritan Solution* on your Facebook.

7) Regularly post this Twitter-friendly link: http://bit.ly/ck0FfH

8) Contribute to the community with your own personal stories and share with others the experience, strength and hope of recovery from addiction.

9) Write your own review of the book and post it at Amazon or Barnes & Noble.

10) Arrange an Authors' speaking event or conference call for your group or organization.

11) Use the Workbook And Action Guide as a small group study on addiction and addiction recovery in your local church, house of worship, or other book study group or organization.

12) Model the Good Samaritan lifestyle in your relationships!

Appendix
*   *   *
# Additional Resources

Contact the authors:

ShellyBaron.com
shelly@shellybaron.com

Facebook.com/SteveBuelow
SteveBuelow.com
steve@stevebuelow.com

The Samaritan Solution
Is Available in Paperback and eBook Versions
Through SamaritanSolution.com,
Amazon, Barnes and Noble,
And Other National And Online Booksellers.

As discussed in Chapter Seven, there are many Twelve Step fellowship programs available throughout the country– and, indeed, throughout the world. All have in common that they are based on the original founding Steps and Traditions of Alcoholics Anonymous.

As of the printing of this book, the following addresses are accurate sources to obtain more information. At any time, a complete list may be obtained by typing *Twelve Step* into the online search engine of your choice.

Here we have provided a few links to national organizations where you may receive details about the programs and services of the most commonly sought-out Twelve Step fellowships:

Alcoholics Anonymous
AA.org

All Addicts Anonymous
AllAddictsAnonymous.org

Al-Anon/Alateen
Al-Anon.Alateen.org

Food Addicts in Recovery Anonymous
FoodAddicts.org

Food Addicts Anonymous
FoodAddictsAnonymous.org

Gamblers Anonymous
GamblersAnonymous.org

GamAnon/Gam-A-Teen
Gam-Anon.org

Narcotics Anonymous
NA.org

Additionally, you may find excellent and useful information and resources from the following faith-based organizations:

Celebrate Recovery
(Combines AA's Twelve Steps and Eight Christian Principles)
CelebrateRecovery.com

JACS
A Program of the Jewish Board of Family and Children's Services
JBFCS.org/JACS

Finally, as new and credible research and resources are made available, you can be sure that we will bring them to you online at:

ShellyBaron.com
SamaritanSolution.com

The Authors

SHELLY BARON is a nationally and internationally recognized expert on identifying and overcoming the disease of addiction.

In private practice for more than 40 years, Shelly has successfully treated over 9000 patients and their loved ones with a comprehensive and unique approach that guides families safely through the minefield of recovery and eliminates the critical mistakes often made in the highly-charged environments surrounding addiction.

Despite having had all the advantages growing up, Shelly nevertheless became an addict. He was raised in a good home with loving parents and grandparents. He had a fine education that included a business degree from New York University. He served our country in the United States Air Force, and gained substantial recognition as a partner in a successful Manhattan advertising firm. Yet, his life spiraled out of control.

By the age of thirty-seven, the partnership at his ad agency was over. His first wife had left him– as had his second– and his children barely knew him. His hands and body were misshapen from rheumatoid arthritis– a result of his addictions. He had also lost all of his hair. Drinking and drugging were part of daily life and he also struggled with food addiction and gambling. One hundred eighty-three pounds heavier than he is today and smoking up to one hundred cigarettes every day, his liver and kidneys were diseased.

That year was 1968. Shelly was examined by four teams of doctors– and given just six months to live. It would take a Samaritan to save his life– and that is exactly what he received.

Today, 40+ years later, Shelly practices and resides in beautiful Boca Raton, Florida and maintains a successful telepractice for those who need his help from a distance.

He is an active member in his community and in his church where he daily proclaims God's goodness, generosity and healing to those victims and families who are seeking true recovery from addiction.

<u>Shelly is a member of:</u>
American Counseling Association
American Mental Health Counselors Association

<u>And holds the following certifications:</u>
Certified Addictions Specialist (CAS)
National Certified Addiction Counselor II (NCAC II)
Credentialed Alcoholism and Substance Abuse Counselor (CASAC)
Licensed Alcohol and Drug Counselor I (LADC I)

ShellyBaron.com
shelly@shellybaron.com

STEVE BUELOW is a successful husband and homeschool dad–and an author, speaker, entrepreneur, mentor and coach who possesses a special ability to weave warmth, humor and common sense into straight-forward, relevant content that delivers powerful messages of inspiration, action, and personal responsibility.

In 1989, amid a crushing financial burden and the fallout from a series of rookie mistakes in a start-up company, Steve began to seek out mentors and to consistently apply powerful leadership and marketing principles that would impact every area of his life and business. Over the next fifteen months, the turnaround would solidify his belief that, regardless of the circumstances, we can always improve our current conditions.

Now, with a passion for helping others achieve what Steve has coined as, "Whole Living," his focus is on co-creating friendships and partnerships that excel physically, spiritually, financially, relationally and emotionally.

To that end, Steve is actively building teams of health- and success-minded men and women as a consultant with one of the fastest growing nutrition and wellness companies in America.

He also continues to personally coach a select group of entrepreneurs and small business leaders, is writing several books, and his online articles, advice, and insights are read by thousands of readers in nearly one hundred countries and all fifty states.

Facebook.com/SteveBuelow
SteveBuelow.com
steve@stevebuelow.com

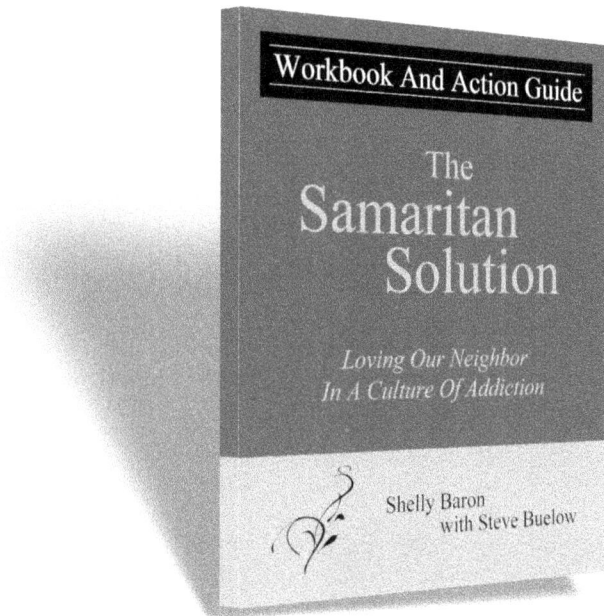

www.ingramcontent.com/pod-product-compliance
Lightning Source LLC
Chambersburg PA
CBHW052032090426
42739CB00010B/1881